The Cognitive and Behavioral Psychology of Project Management

By: B. L. Davidson

Copyright © 2025 B.L. Davidson

All rights reserved. No part of this publication may be reproduced, distributed, or transmitted in any form or by any means, including photocopying, recording, or other electronic or mechanical methods, without the prior written permission of the publisher, except in the case of brief quotations embodied in critical reviews and certain other noncommercial uses permitted by copyright law.

For permission requests, write to the publisher at the address below:

It Was A Dark And Starry Night

5900 Balcones Drive
Austin, TX 78731

info@ITWASADARKANDSTARRYNIGHT.COM

This book is a work of nonfiction. Every effort has been made to ensure that the information contained within is accurate and current as of the date of publication. The author and publisher disclaim responsibility for any errors or omissions and make no representation or warranties regarding the applicability of the ideas or techniques described herein to individual circumstances.

eBook ISBN: 979-8-9987248-0-0
Paperback ISBN: 979-8-9987248-1-7
Hardcover ISBN: 979-8-9987248-2-4

Published by It Was A Dark And Starry Night
Printed in the United States of America

First Edition, April 2025

The Cognitive and Behavioral Psychology of Project Management

~ **B. L. Davidson**

Table of Contents

Preface 1

Chapter 1: The Psychology of Anticipation: Leveraging Insights for Strategic Leadership 4

Chapter 2: The Mindset of a Project Manager 16

Chapter 3: Emotional Intelligence in Leadership 42

Chapter 4: Different Management Styles and Their Psychological Impact 64

Chapter 5: Understanding Team Dynamics 106

Chapter 6: Handling Resistance and Change 135

Chapter 7: Cognitive Load and Time Management 156

Chapter 8: The Physical Price of Stress 183

Conclusion 202

Appendix 205

Glossary 230

Preface

In today's fast-paced and often unpredictable business world, effective project management and leadership are more essential than ever. However, traditional approaches to managing teams, meeting deadlines, and achieving strategic goals often overlook a crucial factor: the psychology behind leadership. This book is designed to bridge that gap, offering an in-depth exploration of the mental and emotional frameworks that shape successful leadership in project management. By understanding and applying principles from psychology, managers and leaders can gain insights that not only enhance productivity and decision-making but also promote a more positive and resilient workplace culture.

The core philosophy of this book is that leadership is as much about managing people as it is about managing projects. When leaders recognize and address the mental and emotional dimensions of their role, they unlock new levels of effectiveness, empathy, and foresight. Rather than focusing solely on technical skills or industry expertise, this book delves into how mindsets, emotions, and interpersonal dynamics influence the success of leaders and their teams. By learning to manage one's mental processes and support those of team members, leaders can foster an environment where creativity, motivation, and productivity can flourish.

Each chapter in this book builds on the psychological foundations of leadership and project management, touching on key aspects such as emotional intelligence, team dynamics, resilience, and cognitive load management. Leaders will find that these chapters reveal the often-hidden elements of successful management and offer actionable insights into handling challenges that arise in today's complex business environment. From understanding how stress impacts physical health to identifying and overcoming cognitive biases, this book provides practical guidance for navigating the psychological demands of leadership.

This book is not simply about understanding others; it is also about deepening self-awareness and fostering growth in one's own leadership journey. Readers will learn strategies for handling their own stress, managing emotional triggers, and setting the mental boundaries necessary for sustainable leadership. Each concept and technique presented is grounded in modern psychological research and designed to be applicable to real-world scenarios that managers face daily.

As you read, you will discover the tools needed to foster a leadership style that is both strategically effective and psychologically sound. By integrating these psychological insights with project management practices, you can develop a balanced approach to leadership that enhances your ability to navigate challenges, drive team performance, and achieve long-term goals.

I hope this book serves as a guide for leaders at every level, offering insights that empower you to lead with greater clarity, compassion, and resilience. Thank you for taking this journey into the psychology of leadership; may it provide you with the knowledge and confidence to lead in ways that are not only effective but also human-centered.

Chapter 1
The Psychology of Anticipation: Leveraging Insights for Strategic Leadership

Organizational and industrial psychology serves as a cornerstone for understanding and enhancing workplace dynamics, particularly for those in leadership roles. This field focuses on applying psychological principles to real-world challenges within professional environments, enabling managers to better understand how individuals and teams function, interact, and perform. By leveraging these insights, leaders can create workspaces that not only foster productivity but also promote emotional well-being and organizational harmony. This chapter delves deeply into these principles, offering a comprehensive exploration of how psychological frameworks can be applied to optimize team performance and guide effective management strategies.

At its core, organizational and industrial psychology helps leaders identify and address the myriad of factors that influence workplace behavior. These factors range from individual differences in personality and motivation to broader organizational influences such as culture, structure, and communication patterns. Understanding these variables equips managers with the tools to recognize and address both visible and underlying issues within their teams. By doing so, they can better predict challenges and implement proactive solutions rather than merely reacting to problems as they arise. This strategic foresight is critical in maintaining a high-functioning team and ensuring long-term organizational success.

The psychological underpinnings of leadership provide valuable insights into how managers can influence, inspire, and direct their teams. Leadership, at its best, is a balance between understanding individual needs and aligning them with organizational objectives. Organizational and industrial psychology sheds light on this balance by examining the motivational factors that drive employees and the stressors that can hinder them. Armed with this knowledge, leaders can design strategies to mitigate workplace stress, prevent burnout, and create a supportive environment where employees feel valued and engaged. This approach is not only humane but also practical, as it leads to higher productivity, lower turnover, and greater overall satisfaction among team members.

Furthermore, this chapter emphasizes the importance of psychological awareness in addressing disruptive behaviors that can destabilize a team. Disruptions—whether in the form of interpersonal conflicts, resistance to change, or declining morale—can erode trust and impede progress. Organizational and industrial psychology offers frameworks for identifying the root causes of such disruptions, enabling leaders to address them effectively and constructively. Rather than allowing conflicts to fester, managers can use these insights to mediate disputes, rebuild relationships, and restore harmony within the team.

Training and development are another critical focus, highlighting how psychological principles can be used to nurture individual success. Effective training goes beyond imparting technical skills; it involves cultivating emotional intelligence, resilience, and adaptability—qualities that are essential for thriving in today's fast-paced and often unpredictable work environments. By integrating psychological insights into training programs, leaders can help employees unlock their potential, overcome challenges, and contribute meaningfully to the team's goals.

Forecasting allows leaders to anticipate future needs, identify potential obstacles, and make informed decisions about how to allocate resources and support their teams. For example, by recognizing patterns in stress levels or workload distribution, managers can adjust priorities to prevent burnout and ensure sustained productivity. This proactive approach not only benefits individual employees but also aligns the team's efforts with broader organizational objectives.

By embracing the principles of organizational and industrial psychology, leaders can move beyond surface-level management to a deeper understanding of their teams. They can create environments that not only drive performance but also prioritize well-being, ensuring that both individuals and organizations thrive. This holistic approach to leadership is not just a strategy for success—it is a blueprint for building resilient, adaptive, and cohesive teams capable of achieving extraordinary results.

Behavioral Blueprint of the Workplace

Understanding workplace behavior requires a psychological lens that penetrates beyond the individuals' obvious actions and interactions. It calls for a deeper exploration of the cognitive and emotional forces that drive behavior within a team setting. At the heart of this analysis lies the concept of the *behavioral blueprint*—a map of how individuals think, feel, and act in response to their environment, peers, and leaders. This intricate map is informed by foundational psychological frameworks, such as personality theories, behavioral models, and motivational drivers, which collectively shape the dynamics of any workplace.

Every workplace is an ecosystem of unique personalities, each bringing their own strengths, weaknesses, and idiosyncrasies. Personality assessments, such as the Big Five Model or the Myers-Briggs Type Indicator (MBTI), offer valuable insights into these differences. They allow leaders to understand what drives each team member, from their preference for structured versus flexible tasks to their approach to risk and decision-making. For example, while some individuals thrive in highly collaborative environments, others may excel when given autonomy and space to innovate independently. Recognizing and respecting these differences enables managers to create tailored management strategies that align with individual preferences, fostering a sense of value and inclusivity.

Behavioral theories also play a critical role in deciphering workplace dynamics. Operant conditioning, for instance, highlights how positive reinforcement can encourage desired behaviors while understanding the consequences of negative reinforcement or punishment helps leaders avoid unintended demotivation. Similarly, social learning theory underscores the importance of modeling appropriate behaviors. When leaders exemplify transparency, accountability, and resilience, their teams are more likely to adopt these qualities. By consciously shaping the behavioral norms of a team, managers can create an environment that promotes cooperation, respect, and innovation.

Motivational models further enrich the behavioral blueprint by providing insights into what drives individuals to perform at their best. Abraham Maslow's hierarchy of needs emphasizes the importance of addressing basic physiological and safety needs before higher-order motivations like self-actualization can be achieved. In a workplace context, this means ensuring fair compensation, job security, and a supportive environment before expecting employees to embrace creativity and innovation. Herzberg's two-factor theory, meanwhile, distinguishes between hygiene factors (e.g., salary, work conditions) that prevent dissatisfaction and motivators (e.g., recognition, meaningful work) that drive satisfaction and engagement. Managers who understand these dynamics can craft roles and responsibilities that align with their team's intrinsic and extrinsic motivators.

Beyond understanding individual behavior, the behavioral blueprint also illuminates patterns and trends within the team as a whole. This macro-level perspective allows leaders to identify potential conflicts before they escalate. For example, clashing work styles or communication gaps can often be predicted through a careful analysis of team interactions and personalities. By addressing these issues proactively—perhaps through conflict resolution training, role adjustments, or fostering open dialogue—managers can maintain harmony and prevent disruptions to productivity.

Furthermore, the behavioral blueprint equips leaders with the tools to adapt their strategies in real-time. In today's fast-paced, ever-changing work environments, agility is key. Managers must be able to pivot their approaches as new challenges and opportunities arise. By understanding the psychological drivers behind the behavior, they can make informed decisions about how to motivate their teams, manage stress, and sustain morale during periods of uncertainty.

Ultimately, the behavioral blueprint is not just a diagnostic tool; it is a foundation for building a more cohesive, adaptable, and high-performing team. When leaders invest time in understanding the psychological nuances of their workplace, they gain the ability to lead with empathy and precision. They can transform challenges into opportunities for growth and create an environment where every team member feels understood, valued, and empowered to contribute. As this understanding deepens, it unlocks the potential for a workplace culture that is not only productive but also psychologically safe, inspiring individuals to reach new heights both personally and professionally. This nuanced approach to leadership is what sets exceptional managers apart, and it is a skill set that will only grow in importance as workplaces become more complex and diverse.

Psychological Forecasting for Strategic Leadership

Effective leadership goes beyond solving problems as they arise; it requires foresight, strategy, and the ability to anticipate challenges before they manifest. This capacity to predict and prepare is where psychological forecasting becomes an indispensable tool for strategic leadership. Rooted in organizational and industrial psychology, psychological forecasting enables leaders to use behavioral and cognitive insights to foresee the trajectory of their teams, predict challenges, and implement proactive solutions. By employing tools like psychometric analysis, stress evaluation, and cultural assessments, leaders can transition from reactive management to a forward-thinking approach that ensures long-term success.

At its core, psychological forecasting draws from the rich data provided by assessments of individual and team dynamics. Psychometric tools, such as personality tests and emotional intelligence evaluations, help leaders understand their team's cognitive styles, motivational drivers, and interpersonal tendencies. For instance, knowing which team members thrive under pressure and which may falter allows for strategic workload distribution. This ensures that high-stakes tasks are assigned to those with the psychological resilience to handle them while others are positioned in roles where they can excel without undue stress. These insights are not just about optimizing performance; they also foster a sense of alignment and fairness within the team, which can significantly enhance morale and engagement.

Stress evaluation is another critical aspect of psychological forecasting. Chronic stress is one of the most pervasive threats to workplace productivity and individual well-being. By implementing tools to measure stress levels—whether through surveys, physiological indicators, or behavioral observations—leaders can identify early warning signs of burnout or disengagement. For example, increased absenteeism, reduced participation in meetings, or noticeable changes in demeanor may signal that an employee is nearing their breaking point. Recognizing these signs early enables leaders to intervene with appropriate support measures, such as workload adjustments, access to counseling, or team-building activities that restore balance and cohesion.

Cultural assessments offer yet another layer of predictive power. Every team operates within a unique cultural framework shaped by its values, norms, and shared experiences. By evaluating this culture, leaders can identify potential sources of friction or alignment. For instance, a team with a strong emphasis on collaboration may struggle to integrate a highly independent new hire without proper onboarding and adjustment strategies. Similarly, understanding the cultural compatibility between different departments or external partners can inform decisions about project assignments and cross-functional initiatives. Aligning team culture with organizational goals is a nuanced process, but it is essential for sustainable success.

One of the most transformative aspects of psychological forecasting is its ability to guide conflict resolution. Many workplace conflicts arise from mismatched expectations, communication gaps, or differences in working styles. By predicting these friction points, leaders can establish systems to address them before they escalate. For example, pairing team members with complementary skills and temperaments can reduce misunderstandings and foster synergy. Establishing clear channels for feedback and dialogue ensures that issues are addressed constructively and in real-time.

Ultimately, psychological forecasting empowers leaders to adopt a proactive rather than reactive management style. It equips them with the knowledge to make informed decisions about team composition, role assignments, and leadership strategies. Rather than waiting for challenges to derail progress, leaders can create contingency plans that account for human factors as well as technical or operational ones. This forward-thinking approach not only minimizes disruptions but also positions teams to seize opportunities with confidence and agility.

By leveraging psychological data and insights, leaders can cultivate an environment where individuals and teams thrive. They can anticipate not just what might go wrong but also what might go right—and then create the conditions for success to unfold. Psychological forecasting is more than a tool for managing the present; it is a vision for shaping the future of leadership, where understanding human behavior is as critical to success as any financial or operational strategy. In a world that demands adaptability and resilience, leaders who master psychological forecasting will stand out as innovators and stewards of lasting progress.

Case Study 1: Creating a Behavioral Blueprint for Workplace Dynamics

Scenario:

Emily has recently been promoted to manage a diverse team with varying personalities and work styles. She notices recurring conflicts between two team members: one prefers structured, step-by-step processes, while the other thrives on improvisation and creativity. Emily needs to create a behavioral blueprint for her team to identify individual strengths, minimize friction, and enhance collaboration.

Questions:

1. How can Emily use personality assessments or behavioral theories to analyze the dynamics between her team members?

2. What strategies can she implement to align individual work styles with the team's overall objectives?

3. How might identifying patterns in team behavior help Emily predict and prevent future conflicts?

Case Study 2: Leveraging Psychological Forecasting for Strategic Decision-Making

Scenario:

Alex, a project manager, is tasked with leading a high-stakes project for a new product launch. He knows that unexpected challenges, such as supply chain disruptions or resource shortages, could derail the timeline. To prepare, Alex decides to use psychological forecasting to anticipate potential risks and allocate resources effectively.

Questions:

1. What tools or methods can Alex use to forecast potential challenges and their impact on the project?

2. How might cognitive biases, such as overconfidence or anchoring, affect his ability to predict risks accurately?

3. What steps can Alex take to ensure his forecasting insights are actionable and communicated effectively to his team?

Case Study 3: Balancing Long-Term Vision with Immediate Team Needs

Scenario:

Maya, a department leader, is working on a strategic plan to increase her team's productivity over the next year. However, she notices that her team is currently struggling with workload management and morale. Maya must balance addressing immediate team needs while staying focused on the long-term vision for the department.

Questions:

1. How can Maya use anticipatory thinking to address current challenges while aligning them with the department's long-term goals?

2. What psychological factors, such as stress or burnout, might be influencing her team's performance, and how can she mitigate them?

3. How can Maya foster a growth mindset within her team to ensure they remain adaptable and engaged during the planning process?

Reflective Component

After reflecting on the case studies, readers should:

- Consider how they would approach similar challenges in their workplace.

- Identify three key insights from the chapter that could guide their strategies for analyzing workplace behavior and forecasting outcomes.

- Explore how integrating psychological tools, such as personality assessments or scenario planning, could enhance their decision-making.

These case studies reinforce the chapter's focus on behavioral analysis and anticipatory leadership, providing practical scenarios for readers to apply what they've learned.

Chapter 2
The Mindset of a Project Manager

Self-awareness involves having a clear understanding of one's strengths, weaknesses, emotional triggers, and behavioral patterns. For project managers, being self-aware is essential for making informed decisions, managing teams effectively, and maintaining emotional control in high-pressure situations. Being cognizant is not a static trait but rather an ongoing process that requires intentional reflection and continuous improvement. Self-aware leaders are better equipped to navigate uncertainty and complexity. Being aware of personal strengths allows a project manager to leverage them for optimal results. Recognizing weaknesses, on the other hand, enables leaders to delegate tasks, seek support, and invest in personal development where necessary. This balance of strengths and weaknesses ensures that the project manager remains effective, reducing the likelihood of blind spots that can negatively affect team dynamics or project outcomes.

Emotional triggers are another key aspect of self-awareness. In a project management setting, emotional reactions can have significant consequences on team morale and decision-making processes. Understanding what triggers emotional responses, such as frustration or impatience, allows leaders to manage these emotions more effectively. This control is vital for maintaining professional relationships and ensuring clear, rational thinking in stressful situations. By recognizing and regulating emotions, a project manager can create a stable and predictable environment for their team, which fosters trust and confidence.

To cultivate self-awareness, project managers should incorporate reflective practices into their daily routines. One of the most effective techniques for fostering self-awareness is regular self-reflection. This can be done at the end of each day or after key interactions, meetings, or decisions. By taking the time to reflect on what went well, what could have been improved, and how personal actions influenced outcomes, leaders can gain deeper insights into their behavioral patterns. Keeping a leadership journal is another practical method for tracking personal growth. By documenting thoughts, emotions, and behaviors over time, project managers can identify recurring themes or areas that need attention.

Feedback is another essential tool for developing self-awareness. In the modern business world, leaders can access 360-degree feedback systems, where input is collected from supervisors, peers, subordinates, and sometimes clients. This comprehensive feedback provides a well-rounded view of how others perceive the leader's actions, communication style, and overall effectiveness. By reviewing this feedback objectively, project managers can compare external perceptions with their own self-assessment, helping to identify discrepancies that may not have been apparent

Additionally, mindfulness practices are gaining traction as a method for enhancing self-awareness. By practicing mindfulness, project managers can become more attuned to their thoughts and emotions in the present moment, which reduces impulsivity and increases emotional regulation. Simple practices such as deep breathing or short meditation sessions can be integrated into a busy workday, helping leaders remain calm and focused.

Ultimately, self-awareness allows project managers to lead with authenticity, aligning their actions with their core values and principles. It builds credibility and fosters a culture of openness and trust within the team. In an environment where communication, collaboration, and conformity are critical to success, self-awareness is not just a desirable trait but a foundational aspect of leadership excellence.

Cognitive Flexibility

Cognitive flexibility is the mental ability to adapt to new information, shifting demands, or changing circumstances. In project management, where unpredictability and complexity are inherent, cognitive flexibility becomes an essential skill. It requires a project manager to remain open to new perspectives, reevaluate previously held assumptions, and alter strategies as necessary. This flexibility allows leaders to respond effectively to unexpected changes and maintain progress toward project goals despite evolving conditions.

Cognitive flexibility involves the capacity to switch between different mental frameworks integrating new information while reassessing current approaches. This process requires breaking free from rigid thinking patterns and avoiding the cognitive trap of confirmation bias, where one seeks out information that only reinforces pre-existing beliefs. Leaders with cognitive flexibility demonstrate adaptability by regularly updating their mental models to align with new data or environmental changes. They are not attached to a single way of thinking or doing things but instead show a willingness to learn and apply different approaches depending on the situation.

In contrast, cognitive inflexibility is characterized by a resistance to change, a reluctance to entertain new ideas, and an unwillingness to deviate from established plans. Individuals who are cognitively inflexible tend to be stubborn and dismissive of perspectives that challenge their own. This rigidity can lead to decision-making paralysis, where a project manager is unable or unwilling to pivot strategies when faced with changing circumstances. It can also create an atmosphere where team members feel stifled or unvalued, as their input is disregarded in favor of maintaining the status quo. Over time, this inflexibility can result in suboptimal project outcomes, as the leader is unable to capitalize on opportunities or address emergent risks in a timely manner.

To embrace cognitive flexibility, project managers must cultivate an openness to new information and practice the deliberate examination of their own thought processes. This starts with a willingness to question assumptions and recognize that no solution is ever static. Cognitive reappraisal, a psychological technique where individuals reinterpret a situation to view it from a different angle, is a critical skill for fostering flexibility. This reappraisal process helps project managers step back from an emotionally charged situation, view it objectively, and consider alternative approaches without being swayed by initial reactions or entrenched beliefs.

Another key element of cognitive flexibility is divergent thinking, which is the ability to generate multiple solutions to a given problem. In project management, this means brainstorming various strategies and approaches rather than locking into a single path. Divergent thinking encourages creativity and innovation, allowing project managers to navigate complex problems by considering all available options. Leaders who can pivot between divergent and convergent thinking—where they narrow down those options to select the best course of action—are better equipped to adapt to new challenges.

Embracing cognitive flexibility means accepting that uncertainty is a natural part of any project and recognizing that rigid adherence to predetermined plans can hinder progress. It involves staying curious, continuously seeking out new perspectives, and being willing to adjust strategies when new information becomes available. For a project manager, this flexibility leads to improved decision-making, enhanced problem-solving abilities, and the capacity to lead a team through rough situations with confidence, making the journey as comfortable as possible for everyone in the whole team.

Incorporating cognitive flexibility into daily project management practices not only enhances personal leadership effectiveness but also fosters a team culture that values change, innovation, and collaboration. In a business environment where change is constant, those who embrace cognitive flexibility are better positioned to achieve long-term success.

The Four Components of Emotional Intelligence

Cultivating Emotional Intelligence (EQ) allows leaders to manage both themselves and others with greater effectiveness. Emotional intelligence comprises four core components: self-awareness, self-regulation, empathy, and social skills. Each of these elements plays a crucial role in the day-to-day interactions of a project manager, contributing to more effective communication, leadership, and team cohesion. While we have already discussed the importance of self-awareness, we will now dive a little deeper into this concept, along with a closer examination of self-regulation, empathy, and social skills. Understanding these components and developing specific strategies to enhance each can significantly improve the overall management of projects.

Self-awareness is the foundation of emotional intelligence. It refers to a leader's ability to recognize and understand their own emotions, as well as the impact those emotions have on their decision-making and behavior. A self-aware project manager is attuned to how their emotional state affects interactions with team members and stakeholders. This awareness is critical for maintaining professionalism and ensuring that personal biases or emotional reactions do not interfere with rational decision-making. To cultivate self-awareness, project managers should practice regular reflection. This can be done through journaling or taking time to mentally review their emotional responses to specific situations, especially after key meetings or interactions. Developing a habit of checking in with oneself, asking questions like, "What am I feeling right now?" or "How is this emotion influencing my behavior?" can help foster a deeper awareness of emotions and their impact on leadership.

Self-regulation is the ability to manage and control emotional reactions, particularly in stressful situations. A project manager with strong self-regulation skills can respond calmly and constructively, even when facing unexpected challenges or conflicts. This ability to remain composed and level-headed is critical in maintaining a professional and productive work environment. Enhancing self-regulation requires practicing mindfulness and emotional control techniques. One effective method is practicing deep breathing or mindfulness meditation to improve the ability to stay centered during stressful moments. Another approach is to pause before reacting to emotionally charged situations, allowing for a moment of reflection before responding. This pause helps mitigate impulsive reactions that can damage relationships or escalate conflicts within the team.

Empathy involves understanding and being sensitive to the emotions, needs, and perspectives of others. In project management, empathy is essential for building trust and fostering strong working relationships with team members and stakeholders. A highly empathetic project manager can recognize when someone is struggling or frustrated and adjust their approach to offer support or guidance as needed. To cultivate empathy, project managers should actively practice perspective-taking, which involves consciously trying to see situations from the other person's viewpoint. Asking open-ended questions that invite team members to share their thoughts and feelings also helps build empathy. Additionally, focusing on active listening—fully concentrating, understanding, and responding appropriately—can enhance empathetic communication and strengthen team bonds.

Social skills refer to the ability to manage relationships, navigate social complexities, and influence others effectively. For project managers, this includes communication, conflict resolution, and the ability to inspire and lead a team. Strong social skills are necessary for motivating team members, facilitating collaboration, and managing stakeholder relationships. To develop social skills, project managers should focus on improving their communication style. This can involve practicing clear, concise, and direct communication while remaining open to feedback. Another strategy is to hone conflict resolution skills by learning how to mediate disagreements constructively and maintain a positive atmosphere during team discussions.

Regularly seeking opportunities to engage with others socially—whether through informal conversations or structured team-building activities—also helps build rapport and strengthen leadership presence. Techniques such as mindfulness training, active listening, and regular reflection are crucial for enhancing self-awareness, self-regulation, empathy, and social skills. By focusing on these areas, project managers can cultivate an emotionally intelligent leadership style that improves team dynamics, fosters better communication, and leads to more successful project outcomes. Emotional intelligence, when fully developed, allows leaders to manage themselves and others with greater empathy, resilience, and effectiveness, ultimately enhancing both individual and team performance.

Building Psychological Resilience

It is a necessity for project managers to thrive in the demanding and unpredictable environment of project management, which is why proven psychological resiliency should be a prerequisite. Resilience refers to the ability to adapt, recover, and maintain mental well-being in the face of adversity, setbacks, and stress. The human brain has a remarkable capacity to heal itself, known as neuroplasticity, which enables individuals to recover from difficult situations and grow stronger over time. This mental toughness is not just a personal asset but also a key leadership trait that can be modeled to foster a resilient team culture.

Developing resilience as a project manager requires a deliberate shift in mindset. It begins with recognizing that setbacks and failures are inevitable in any complex project. However, instead of viewing them as permanent or insurmountable, resilient leaders perceive challenges as opportunities for growth and learning. This mindset shift, grounded in cognitive reframing, allows project managers to maintain a solution-focused approach even when faced with significant obstacles. By reframing negative events in a more neutral or positive light, the brain is trained to respond with resilience, avoiding emotional exhaustion and fostering a sense of control.

The power of the human brain to adapt is supported by research. Studies, such as those conducted by psychologists like Dr. Martin Seligman, a pioneer of positive psychology, have shown that resilience can be learned and strengthened through certain cognitive and behavioral techniques. Seligman's work demonstrated that individuals who develop an optimistic explanatory style—viewing setbacks as temporary, specific, and external—are more likely to bounce back from adversity than those who adopt a pessimistic outlook. This research underscores the importance of mindset in psychological resilience, which can directly impact how project managers handle high-pressure situations and setbacks.

Building psychological resilience involves adopting a proactive approach to stress management and mental well-being. This includes maintaining mental clarity under pressure by practicing mindfulness or meditation, which helps regulate the brain's stress response. By engaging in these practices, project managers can remain focused and composed during crises, ensuring that their decision-making remains sharp and balanced. Additionally, project managers should prioritize self-care routines, including adequate rest, exercise, and mental breaks, as part of their strategy to build and maintain resilience. These practices help to keep the brain and body in optimal condition, ready to handle the challenges that arise in a project. A project manager's resilience has a direct impact on the team. When a leader models psychological toughness, calmness, and an optimistic attitude, it sets the tone for the team to follow. Resilient leaders demonstrate that setbacks are part of the process, encouraging the team to remain focused on solutions rather than problems. In project management, this translates to maintaining team morale, keeping productivity high, and preventing burnout when projects do not go as planned. Through consistent modeling of resilient behaviors, a project manager can instill resilience within the team, creating a group dynamic where individuals feel empowered to face challenges head-on and adapt to unforeseen changes without losing motivation.

Building psychological resilience is a vital skill for project managers aiming to thrive under pressure and guide their teams through challenging projects. By understanding the brain's ability to heal and adapt, applying cognitive strategies like reframing, and incorporating proactive stress-management techniques, project managers can develop the mental toughness required to lead effectively. In turn, by modeling resilience, they can cultivate a team culture that thrives on perseverance and a forward-looking mindset, ensuring long-term project success.

The Growth Mindset

The growth mindset is a crucial psychological framework for project managers who need to navigate the complexities and challenges inherent in project management. Coined by psychologist Carol Dweck, the growth mindset is based on the belief that abilities and intelligence can be developed through effort, learning, and perseverance. This mindset contrasts with a fixed mindset, where individuals believe that their abilities are static and unchangeable. For project managers, adopting a growth mindset is essential for viewing challenges not as insurmountable obstacles but as opportunities for growth, learning, and improvement.

Human motivation for growth and overcoming challenges is evident from the early stages of development. Studies on infant behavior, such as research by developmental psychologists, show that babies display a remarkable drive to overcome obstacles. They are motivated to achieve goals, such as learning to walk or communicate, despite numerous failures and setbacks. Babies consistently try, fail, and try again without discouragement, demonstrating a natural resilience and belief in their capacity for improvement. This early-life behavior suggests that humans are innately inclined toward growth and mastery, but as individuals age, environmental factors, experiences, and personal beliefs can either nurture or stifle this drive.

As adults, some people continue to embrace challenges as opportunities for growth, while others avoid them out of fear of failure or the discomfort of change. In a project management setting, having a growth mindset is vital for success. A project manager who views challenges as opportunities understands that every setback or difficulty is an occasion to learn, adapt, and refine strategies. This mindset encourages experimentation, creativity, and perseverance, all of which are necessary when managing projects with high levels of uncertainty and complexity.

In contrast, a project manager with a fixed mindset may see challenges as threats to their competence, avoid taking risks, and shy away from new opportunities. This circumvention can stifle innovation, limit team growth, and impede project success. If challenges are perceived as something to be feared or avoided, both the project manager and their team can become stagnant, sticking to familiar approaches and becoming less adaptable in the face of new or evolving demands. A project manager cannot afford to run from opportunities, even if they come disguised as challenges. To lead effectively, they must embrace the idea that growth comes through effort, and that failure is not a dead end but a stepping stone toward eventual success. For project managers, cultivating a growth mindset involves rethinking how they approach difficulties. Instead of viewing failures as personal shortcomings, they should see them as learning experiences that offer valuable insights into how to improve. This mindset fosters resilience, as challenges are no longer perceived as negative events but as essential components of the learning and development process. Additionally, a growth-oriented project manager will inspire their team to adopt the same attitude, creating an environment where continuous improvement, flexibility, and innovation are prioritized over rigid adherence to perfection.

In the context of project management, where unforeseen challenges are inevitable, the ability to embrace a growth mindset can determine the overall success of a project. It allows project managers to remain flexible, adjust strategies as needed, and continuously improve their leadership and management skills. Moreover, by modeling a growth mindset, they encourage their team members to stay motivated and resilient, even when faced with setbacks. Challenges should be seen as opportunities to refine approaches, strengthen team dynamics, and improve both individual and collective performance. By fostering this mindset within themselves and their teams, project managers create an atmosphere of growth, resilience, and continuous development, which is crucial in today's business world.

Avoiding Cognitive Biases

Cognitive biases are systematic errors in thinking that can distort perception and lead to flawed conclusions. In project management, where decisions are frequently made under uncertainty and pressure, the ability to recognize and mitigate these biases is critical for maintaining objectivity and optimizing outcomes. Confirmation bias, one of the most common mental pitfalls, occurs when individuals selectively seek out or prioritize information that confirms their preexisting beliefs while ignoring evidence that contradicts them. Project managers must remain vigilant against this bias by actively challenging their assumptions and seeking diverse viewpoints to ensure all relevant information is considered. This practice fosters a more balanced and objective analysis, reducing the risk of misguided decisions.

Overconfidence bias is another cognitive trap where individuals overestimate their knowledge, skills, or the accuracy of their predictions. This can lead to unrealistic expectations and flawed project estimates. To mitigate overconfidence, project managers should incorporate structured feedback processes and regularly consult with their teams and external experts to validate assumptions and adjust forecasts accordingly. The planning fallacy, a bias that causes people to underestimate the time, costs, and risks involved in completing a project, is particularly detrimental in project management. To counter this, managers should adopt a more conservative approach by incorporating contingency plans and padding estimates to account for unforeseen challenges. Periodically reviewing progress and adjusting timelines helps maintain realistic project expectations.

Reducing these mental pitfalls fosters a clearer understanding of project challenges and opportunities, ultimately contributing to better project outcomes. By actively identifying and mitigating cognitive biases, project managers can enhance the quality of their decisions, improve judgment, and lead projects more effectively.

Balancing Assertiveness and Empathy

Assertiveness allows a leader to communicate their expectations clearly and maintain control over the project, while empathy fosters trust and strong interpersonal relationships. Striking the right balance between these two qualities is essential for effective leadership without alienating team members or compromising on standards.

In a project management setting, consider a scenario where a project manager notices a team member consistently missing deadlines. The manager needs to address the issue to keep the project on track, but an aggressive approach could harm the relationship and demotivate the team member. An empathetic leader might acknowledge the personal struggles or workload pressures the team member may be facing, but an overly accommodating response would risk setting a precedent for leniency. To find the right balance, the manager could assertively express the importance of meeting deadlines for the success of the project, while empathetically inquiring if there are any specific challenges preventing the team member from completing tasks on time. By offering support while maintaining firm expectations, the manager shows both understanding and leadership.

In another scenario, a project manager must negotiate with a client who is demanding unrealistic changes late in the project. Being too assertive might jeopardize the client relationship, while being too accommodating would put undue pressure on the team and the project timeline. Here, the project manager can assertively explain the constraints, highlighting the impact on scope, time, and resources. At the same time, they can empathetically acknowledge the client's concerns and offer alternative solutions that align with the project's capabilities. This approach reinforces the manager's leadership by setting boundaries while maintaining a collaborative and respectful dialogue.

Project managers should aim to lead through influence rather than solely relying on authority. Balancing assertiveness and empathy create an environment where leadership is respected and relationships are strengthened.

Developing a Long-Term Vision

Long-term strategic thinking allows managers to stay focused on overarching goals and ensure that short-term challenges do not derail the project's ultimate objectives. It requires the ability to see beyond immediate issues and maintain a clear sense of direction, aligning daily decisions with the broader vision of the project. In project management, it is easy to become consumed by the constant stream of daily tasks, emergencies, and unforeseen complications. While addressing these is crucial for the smooth functioning of the project, it is equally important not to lose sight of the larger objectives. A long-term vision serves as a compass, guiding decisions and prioritizing actions that contribute to sustainable success. Project managers must cultivate the ability to rise above the immediate demands and view problems through the lens of long-term impact and overall project trajectory.

Staying focused on the big picture requires discipline and resilience. The pressure to resolve immediate concerns can lead to reactive decision-making, which may satisfy short-term needs but harm the project in the long run. Project managers must continually ask themselves how each decision aligns with the broader vision, ensuring that short-term solutions do not compromise long-term objectives. This strategic thinking also helps to anticipate future challenges and proactively plan for them, rather than being constantly caught off guard by unexpected issues.

Therefore, in order for project managers to navigate the complexities of both strategic planning and daily operations, they must develop a long-term vision. Maintaining long-term focus amid short-term challenges involves consistent communication with the team, ensuring that everyone understands the ultimate goals and how their work contributes to them. By reinforcing the long-term vision, project managers can prevent the team from getting bogged down in the minutiae of daily tasks and inspire a sense of purpose that drives sustained progress, even in the face of immediate obstacles.

Managing Stress and Avoiding Burnout

Chronic stress, if left unchecked, can lead to burnout, which negatively affects both the individual and the team. Burnout results in decreased productivity, poor decision-making, and strained relationships. Therefore, it is essential to adopt effective stress management strategies and prioritize work-life balance to prevent long-term psychological damage.

One practical approach is utilizing an Employee Assistance Program (EAP), a work-based intervention program that provides confidential support services, including counseling and resources for stress management. Under the law, employers are often required to provide access to EAPs, which help employees cope with personal or work-related issues that may affect their performance or well-being. By encouraging the use of EAPs, project managers can create a supportive environment that promotes mental health and helps employees address stress before it leads to burnout.

Maintaining a healthy work-life balance is another key factor in preventing stress. Project managers and their teams should prioritize taking regular vacation time, ensuring breaks from work to recharge physically and mentally. Regular visits to healthcare professionals should also be part of one's self-care routine, ensuring that physical health is not neglected. It is critical to avoid placing work demands before one's health, as doing so can lead to serious consequences, including stress-related illnesses.

Project managers must also be able to recognize the signs of stress in themselves and others. Regular, casual conversations with team members can help in pinpointing stress early. By checking in regularly and fostering open communication, managers can identify when someone may be overwhelmed or struggling, offering support before it escalates into burnout. Managing stress and preventing burnout require a holistic approach that prioritizes mental and physical health, encourages the use of supportive resources like EAP, and emphasizes the importance of balance between work and personal life.

Monitoring Self-Sabotaging Behaviors

Perfectionism, procrastination, and imposter syndrome are three common psychological barriers that can derail progress and undermine confidence. These behaviors stem from deep-rooted cognitive and behavioral patterns that project managers must recognize and address to overcome their detrimental effects on both personal performance and team dynamics.

Perfectionism, in particular, is driven by an intense fear of failure and a desire for control. From a behavioral psychology perspective, perfectionism manifests as an escapism, where individuals delay completing tasks or refrain from taking action unless they can achieve an unattainable standard of flawlessness. This is often coupled with cognitive distortions, such as all-or-nothing thinking, where anything less than perfection is seen as failure. Organizational psychology teaches that perfectionism can lead to inefficiencies in project management, as excessive attention to detail or unrealistic standards may result in missed deadlines, micromanagement, and a demotivated team. By recognizing this pattern, project managers can begin to shift their focus from perfect outcomes to progress and learning, fostering a more realistic and adaptable mindset.

Procrastination, another self-sabotaging behavior, often occurs as a result of psychological resistance to stress or discomfort associated with a particular task. From a cognitive-behavioral standpoint, procrastination is reinforced through avoidance, where individuals experience temporary relief by postponing complex tasks. However, this perpetuates a cycle of stress and inefficiency, leading to increased anxiety and last-minute rushes that compromise the quality of work. Organizational psychology emphasizes the importance of time management and prioritization in combating procrastination. Project managers should develop self-awareness of their procrastination triggers and implement strategies such as task segmentation, deadline setting, and accountability to break the procrastination cycle and increase productivity.

Imposter syndrome is another form of self-sabotage, where individuals feel inadequate despite evident competence and accomplishments. This cognitive distortion leads project managers to doubt their abilities, fearing that they will be exposed as frauds. Imposter syndrome can result in overcompensating behaviors such as taking on too much responsibility or, conversely, withdrawing from opportunities to avoid failure. Organizational psychology suggests that imposter syndrome can disrupt leadership effectiveness, as it can cause project managers to undermine their authority, second-guess decisions, and over-rely on external validation. To overcome imposter syndrome, project managers need to reframe their internal dialogue, recognizing that their expertise and qualifications are valid. Seeking feedback and acknowledging accomplishments are key strategies to dismantle the negative self-talk associated with imposter syndrome.

Monitoring these self-sabotaging behaviors requires a strong sense of self-awareness and an ability to identify underlying cognitive distortions. Organizational psychology offers valuable insights into how behaviors such as perfectionism, procrastination, and imposter syndrome impact team dynamics and productivity. By understanding these psychological traps, project managers can take proactive steps to counteract them. This involves implementing strategies for cognitive restructuring, where negative or irrational thought patterns are challenged and replaced with more realistic, growth-oriented perspectives. Behavioral strategies, such as setting achievable goals, breaking down large tasks, and practicing self-compassion, also play a crucial role in mitigating these tendencies.

By addressing perfectionism, procrastination, and imposter syndrome through both cognitive and behavioral strategies, project managers can break free from the cycle of self-sabotage and lead with greater confidence, efficiency, and resilience.

Try This: Actionable Steps for Developing the Project Manager Mindset

1. Strengthen Cognitive Flexibility

- Exercise: Start your day by challenging yourself to consider alternative perspectives on a current work issue. For example, ask yourself, *"How might a different team member view this problem?"* or *"What would happen if we approached this task differently?"*

- Action: Regularly rotate tasks or roles within your team (if feasible) to force yourself and others to adapt to new challenges and perspectives.

2. Master Emotional Intelligence

- Self-Awareness: Spend five minutes daily journaling about your emotional reactions to workplace events. Note what triggered your feelings and how you responded.

- Self-Regulation: Practice "pause and respond." When you feel triggered, take three deep breaths before reacting. Use that moment to choose a measured response.

- Empathy: Commit to one "active listening" session per day with a colleague. During a conversation, focus solely on understanding their perspective without interrupting or judging.

- Social Skills: Reach out to a colleague you don't often interact with and schedule a brief coffee chat. Building these connections strengthens your relational network.

3. Build Psychological Resilience

- Exercise: Develop a list of your core values and reflect on how they align with your current role. This helps you anchor your decisions and manage stress during challenging times.

- Action: Practice mindfulness or meditation for 5–10 minutes daily to improve focus and reduce emotional reactivity. Apps like Calm or Headspace can help.

4. Foster a Growth Mindset

- Exercise: Write down one area where you feel challenged or stuck. Reframe it as an opportunity for growth by identifying one thing you can learn from the situation.

- Action: Commit to learning something new related to your field each month. This could include reading an article, attending a webinar, or taking a short online course.

5. Combat Cognitive Biases

- Exercise: Before making decisions, deliberately seek out information or perspectives that challenge your initial assumptions. This "devil's advocate" approach reduces confirmation bias.

- Action: Create a checklist for major decisions that includes prompts like:
  - Have I considered alternative perspectives?
  - What evidence contradicts my assumptions?
  - How might my biases be influencing this decision?

6. Balance Assertiveness and Empathy

- Exercise: Practice using "I" statements in conversations to express your needs assertively without sounding aggressive. For example, *"I need more detailed feedback to improve my work on this project."*

- Action: Observe your team's emotional dynamics during meetings. Aim to assert your viewpoint and validate others' feelings by saying things like, *"I see where you're coming from, and I think we can also consider..."*

7. Develop a Long-Term Vision

- Exercise: Create a vision board for your current project or career. Include goals, milestones, and the values you want to uphold. Reflect on this vision weekly to stay aligned with your objectives.

- Action: Break your long-term goals into smaller, actionable steps. Use tools like SMART goals (Specific, Measurable, Achievable, Relevant, Time-Bound) to track progress.

8. Manage Stress and Avoid Burnout

- Exercise: Start a weekly stress inventory. Note what caused stress, how you managed it, and what you can do to prevent similar stressors in the future.

- Action: Schedule regular "non-negotiable" breaks into your day, even if it's just 10 minutes to stretch or take a quick walk. Small breaks boost mental clarity and resilience.

9. Monitor and Address Self-Sabotaging Behaviors

- Exercise: Identify one habit that might be holding you back, such as procrastination or negative self-talk. Create a replacement habit. For example, replace *"I can't do this"* with *"I'll break this into smaller steps."*

- Action: Ask a trusted colleague or mentor to hold you accountable for overcoming this habit. Check in weekly to discuss progress.

Reflect and Revisit

Remember, building the mindset of a successful project manager is a continuous journey. Reflect on these exercises regularly and revise them as you grow. If you find yourself facing a particular challenge, revisit this chapter and try a new approach. For a deeper understanding of terms and concepts, refer to the Glossary at the end of the book—it's a resource designed to support your ongoing growth.

With these steps, you're not just reading about effective project management—you're actively shaping yourself into a leader who can inspire, adapt, and excel.

Case Study 1: Adapting to Change with Cognitive Flexibility

Scenario:

Laura, a project manager, has been overseeing a product development project for six months. Midway through the project, the client changes the requirements, introducing new features that will significantly impact the scope and timeline. While her team feels frustrated and overwhelmed, Laura recognizes the importance of quickly adapting to the new reality while maintaining team morale and project progress.

Questions:

1. How can Laura use cognitive flexibility to reframe the situation and guide her team through this change effectively?

2. What steps can Laura take to ensure her team feels supported and motivated during this transition?

3. How might Laura balance short-term task adjustments with the long-term vision of delivering a successful product?

Case Study 2: Developing Emotional Intelligence to Resolve Team Tensions

Scenario:

David manages a diverse team with varying communication styles. Recently, misunderstandings between two team members have escalated into open disagreements, creating tension and slowing project progress. David must rely on his emotional intelligence—particularly self-awareness, empathy, and social skills—to defuse the situation and rebuild team harmony.

Questions:

1. What role does self-awareness play in how David approaches the conflict, and how can it help him set the right tone for resolution?

2. How can David apply empathy to understand the perspectives of the conflicting team members and foster mutual understanding?

3. What specific social skills can David use to mediate the conflict and re-establish collaboration within his team?

Case Study 3: Overcoming Self-Sabotaging Behaviors in Leadership

Scenario:

Sophia, a newly promoted manager, has been struggling with perfectionism. She frequently delays decisions and micromanages her team to ensure every detail is perfect, leading to missed deadlines and team frustration. Sophia realizes her self-sabotaging behaviors are not only impacting her performance but also eroding trust and morale within her team.

Questions:

1. How can Sophia identify the underlying causes of her perfectionism and address them constructively?

2. What strategies could Sophia use to delegate tasks more effectively while overcoming the urge to micromanage?

3. How might adopting a growth mindset help Sophia shift her focus from perfection to continuous improvement and team development?

Reflective Component

I encourage readers to:

- Reflect on similar challenges they have faced and the lessons they've learned.

- Consider how the principles of cognitive flexibility, emotional intelligence, and resilience could have altered outcomes in their scenarios.

- Write down three actionable steps they can take to strengthen their mindset as a project manager, based on the insights gained from these case studies.

This set of case studies ties directly to the themes of Chapter 2, providing readers with practical scenarios to deepen their understanding of the mindset and emotional skills needed for effective leadership.

Chapter 3
Emotional Intelligence in Leadership

Earlier, I mentioned the importance of identifying our emotional triggers; now, we delve deeper into regulating these triggers to maintain composure and compliancy, particularly during stressful situations. Many emotional triggers are deeply rooted, often originating from early life experiences. These triggers may remain unconscious in adulthood, leading individuals to react emotionally without fully understanding why. Such reactions can perpetuate a cycle where individuals feel victimized by their emotions rather than recognizing and managing them. However, these patterns are not immutable; they can be altered with intentional effort and self-awareness.

Self-regulation involves the ability to control one's emotional responses and maintain a balanced state of mind despite external circumstances. From a psychological perspective, this involves several techniques.

Cognitive-behavioral approaches highlight the role of cognitive restructuring, a method that allows individuals to identify and challenge distorted thought patterns that exacerbate emotional reactions. By replacing negative or irrational thoughts with more balanced and realistic ones, leaders can mitigate their emotional responses and respond more effectively to stress.

Behavioral psychology also offers insights into self-regulation through the principle of operant conditioning, which emphasizes the use of reinforcement to encourage desirable behaviors. Leaders can apply this principle by reinforcing positive emotional responses and coping strategies through self-reward or recognition. Additionally, the practice of mindfulness, as introduced by Jon Kabat-Zinn, has been shown to enhance emotional regulation by increasing awareness of present-moment experiences and reducing the impact of negative emotions.

Research has demonstrated the significant impact of emotional regulation on workplace dynamics. Studies, such as those conducted by James Gross, have shown that individuals who effectively manage their emotions are better at coping with stress and maintaining job satisfaction. Gross's research on emotion regulation strategies reveals those techniques like cognitive reappraisal—where individuals change their interpretation of a situation to alter their emotional response—are particularly effective in reducing workplace stress.

The concept of emotional intelligence, as articulated by Daniel Goleman, underscores the importance of self-regulation in leadership. Goleman's framework suggests that leaders who can manage their emotional triggers are more adept at handling interpersonal conflicts, fostering a positive work environment, and leading teams with empathy and understanding. Emotional intelligence involves not just recognizing one's emotions but also employing strategies to control them in ways that enhance leadership effectiveness.

It is important to recognize that everyone carries emotional baggage from previous experiences into new environments. This baggage can manifest as unresolved issues, past traumas, or entrenched behavioral patterns. By acknowledging these influences and actively working to address them, leaders can break the cycle of negative emotional responses. Engaging in reflective practices, seeking feedback, and pursuing professional development opportunities can facilitate this process.

In these ways, leaders can maintain composure under pressure, foster a productive work environment, and enhance their overall effectiveness. Recognizing and addressing the deep-rooted nature of emotional triggers and the impact of past experiences is essential for achieving long-term emotional balance and leadership success.

Cognitive Restructuring

Cognitive restructuring, a core technique in cognitive-behavioral therapy (CBT), involves challenging and changing negative thought patterns that hinder emotional resilience and effectiveness. In leadership, especially in project management, negative self-talk and distorted thinking can create barriers to success. Leaders may unintentionally reinforce harmful beliefs that damage their self-esteem, decision-making abilities, and relationships with colleagues. Cognitive restructuring offers a method to disrupt these destructive thought cycles and replace them with more balanced, rational, and constructive ones, thereby fostering stronger emotional resilience and enhancing leadership capabilities.

A common challenge that leaders face is negative self-talk or irrational beliefs. For instance, a project manager may start believing that every time the executive they report to goes into their office, they are discussing the project manager's performance. This belief might stem from personal insecurities or past experiences where they felt unfairly scrutinized. This type of thinking is referred to as "mind reading"—assuming that others are thinking negatively about you without evidence. In cognitive restructuring, this is classified as a cognitive distortion. It is based on inaccurate or exaggerated perceptions that can lead to unnecessary stress, anxiety, and poor leadership decisions.

Leaders often harbor these cognitive distortions due to underlying insecurities or past experiences. Whether it's fear of failure, perfectionism, or imposter syndrome, such insecurities can lead to assumptions and negative thoughts that cloud judgment and leadership performance. Cognitive restructuring provides a systematic way for leaders to identify and reframe these distorted thoughts, replacing them with more constructive and reality-based perspectives.

The process of cognitive restructuring typically follows a series of steps that leaders can use to reframe their thinking:

1 **Identify the Negative Thought:** The first step in cognitive restructuring is to recognize when a negative or irrational thought arises. A project manager who assumes that others are discussing them behind closed doors can pause and acknowledge this thought. By identifying the negative thought as it occurs, the leader becomes more aware of their internal dialogue and how it affects their emotions and behavior.

2 **Examine the Evidence:** After identifying the thought, the next step is to critically evaluate its accuracy. Is there concrete evidence supporting this belief, or is it based on an assumption? In the case of the project manager who

believes they are being discussed, they might ask themselves whether they've seen or heard anything that confirms this, or if it is merely speculation. Cognitive restructuring encourages individuals to gather objective facts rather than relying on emotions or assumptions.

3 **Challenge the Thought:** Leaders can then challenge the negative thought by considering alternative explanations. In this case, the project manager could consider that the executive might be discussing unrelated business, strategic decisions, or other personnel matters. By introducing alternative, more plausible explanations, the leader can begin to dismantle the grip of the negative thought.

4 **Reframe the Thought:** After challenging the original negative belief, the leader can replace it with a more balanced and realistic one. For example, instead of thinking, "They're always talking about me negatively," the project manager could reframe it as, "There are many reasons for private meetings, and it's unlikely they are always focused on me. I will continue to do my best, regardless of what they discuss."

5 **Test the New Thought:** Finally, cognitive restructuring involves testing the new thought over time. The project manager can observe how they feel after reframing their initial negative assumption. As they practice this regularly, they will likely notice a reduction in stress and anxiety, leading to improved emotional regulation and leadership effectiveness.

Cognitive restructuring is deeply tied to emotional resilience. By reframing negative thoughts, leaders become less reactive to stress and more adaptable in challenging situations. In project management, where uncertainty and high stakes are common, this emotional resilience allows leaders to stay composed, make rational decisions, and maintain positive relationships with their teams. Rather than being driven by insecurity or unfounded assumptions, leaders who practice cognitive restructuring make decisions based on reality and logic.

Research supports the efficacy of cognitive restructuring in reducing anxiety, improving performance, and increasing emotional well-being. Studies have shown that individuals who practice cognitive restructuring techniques regularly experience a significant decrease in negative emotions and cognitive distortions, leading to better workplace performance and leadership outcomes. In the context of leadership, this means more focused decision-making, enhanced problem-solving abilities, and improved communication with team members.

Challenging and reframing negative self-talk and unrealistic beliefs takes some work; however, by doing so, project managers can enhance their emotional resilience, leading to more effective leadership. The steps involved—identifying, examining, challenging, reframing, and testing negative thoughts—provide a structured approach to change thought patterns and ultimately transform how leaders respond to stress, uncertainty, and interpersonal challenges on their team.

Emotional Regulation Theory

Emotional regulation theory examines how individuals influence their own emotional experiences, particularly in stressful or challenging situations. In leadership, the ability to regulate emotions effectively has a direct impact on decision-making, team morale, and overall workplace productivity. Leaders who excel in emotional regulation are better equipped to handle high-pressure scenarios and can create a stable, supportive environment for their teams. Key strategies for emotional regulation include mindfulness, cognitive reappraisal, and adaptive coping mechanisms, all of which enable leaders to manage their emotional responses in a way that benefits both them and those they lead.

Mindfulness is one of the most widely discussed techniques in emotional regulation. It involves maintaining awareness of the present moment without judgment, allowing leaders to observe their emotions without becoming overwhelmed by them. This practice, popularized by Jon Kabat-Zinn, helps leaders develop a non-reactive approach to emotions, reducing impulsivity and promoting calm decision-making. In high-stress environments like project management, where unforeseen challenges are common, mindfulness provides a buffer against emotional overwhelm. By grounding oneself in the present, leaders can approach problems with a clearer, more objective mindset. Mindfulness also promotes emotional intelligence by increasing awareness of both internal emotional states and external social dynamics, fostering better interpersonal interactions.

Cognitive reappraisal, another critical technique, is a form of cognitive restructuring that involves changing the way one interprets emotionally charged situations. Leaders often face situations that trigger negative emotions—whether it's an unexpected project failure or interpersonal conflict. Cognitive reappraisal allows leaders to shift their perspective on these challenges, reframing them in a more constructive light. For example, instead of viewing a project setback as a personal failure, a leader might reappraise it as an opportunity for growth and learning. By altering their interpretation of the event, they can mitigate negative emotions such as frustration, disappointment, or anger and maintain focus on problem-solving. Cognitive reappraisal has been shown in research to be one of the most effective strategies for long-term emotional regulation, as it directly influences the thought patterns that lead to emotional responses.

Adaptive coping mechanisms also play a crucial role in managing stress and maintaining performance. These mechanisms are healthy, constructive strategies that individuals use to cope with stressors rather than avoid or suppress them. Adaptive coping includes techniques like problem-solving, seeking social support, and engaging in physical activity, which can all reduce the emotional burden of stressful situations. In leadership, adopting adaptive coping mechanisms can prevent burnout, improve mental resilience, and maintain motivation during prolonged periods of stress. For instance, a leader facing the pressure of tight deadlines might engage in time management strategies or delegate tasks more effectively, rather than allowing stress to escalate unchecked. By actively addressing the sources of stress, rather than ignoring them, leaders can sustain their performance and well-being over time.

Research in emotional regulation theory, particularly the work of James Gross, emphasizes that emotions are dynamic processes influenced by multiple factors, including situational context, individual personality traits, and learned coping strategies. Gross identifies several stages where emotional regulation can occur, including situation selection (choosing situations that will lead to positive emotions), situation modification (changing aspects of a situation to reduce emotional impact), and response modulation (actively managing emotional responses after they occur). For leaders, this means that emotional regulation is not limited to suppressing or ignoring emotions; rather, it involves proactive strategies for managing emotions before they even arise. Leaders can, for example, select environments or approaches that minimize stress for themselves and their teams or actively modify stressful situations to create a more positive outcome.

Leaders must also be aware of the impact their emotional regulation has on their teams. Emotional contagion, a psychological phenomenon where emotions spread from one individual to others in a group, means that a leader's emotional state can influence the morale and performance of their team. A leader who can regulate their emotions effectively sets a positive tone for their team, encouraging calm, focused behavior even in stressful situations. Conversely, a leader who is reactive or emotionally volatile may inadvertently spread anxiety or frustration, which can undermine team cohesion and performance. Thus, emotional regulation not only benefits the leader but also has a direct impact on the team's dynamics and effectiveness.

Emotional regulation theory provides leaders with a framework for managing their emotions in a way that enhances both personal and organizational performance.

Emotional Contagion and Leadership

Emotional contagion is a psychological phenomenon where emotions spread from one individual to another, influencing group dynamics and the overall atmosphere within a team or organization. In the context of leadership, emotional contagion plays a critical role in shaping workplace culture, morale, and performance. Leaders, by virtue of their authority and visibility, serve as emotional focal points within their teams. The emotions they project can cause a ripple effect throughout the organization, impacting both individual behaviors and collective outcomes. Understanding and managing this process is crucial for leaders who wish to create a motivated and cohesive team environment.

At the core of emotional contagion is the idea that emotions are inherently social, meaning they don't remain confined to the individual experiencing them. Instead, they reverberate through interpersonal interactions, affecting the emotional states of others. This cause-and-effect relationship between one person's emotions and another can lead to the amplification of positive or negative emotional states across a team. For example, when a leader is visibly stressed or frustrated, that emotion can transfer to team members, creating a broader atmosphere of anxiety or dissatisfaction. Conversely, a leader who remains calm and optimistic can instill a sense of confidence and positivity in the group. The reverberation of emotions from leader to team and team members to each other illustrates the power of emotional contagion in the workplace.

Leaders are particularly influential in the emotional dynamics of their teams due to their position of authority and their role in setting the tone for interactions. Their emotional state can trigger a chain reaction, leading to a ripple effect that spreads beyond immediate encounters and permeates the organizational climate. For instance, a leader's negative emotional display during a meeting may cause heightened stress among attendees, which can then carry over into interactions outside the meeting room. This emotional transmission creates a broader impact on the workplace, where one negative moment can have long-lasting effects on team dynamics, performance, and overall morale. The ripple effect is thus a powerful mechanism through which emotions can influence workplace outcomes in both positive and negative ways.

The cause-and-effect relationship inherent in emotional contagion emphasizes that leaders must be mindful of how their emotional states can serve as catalysts for broader emotional experiences within their teams. Emotional expressions, whether verbal or nonverbal, are continuously picked up by team members and can significantly influence how they perceive their work environment, colleagues, and tasks. A leader's consistent display of stress or frustration, for instance, may cause employees to become demoralized or disengaged. On the other hand, a leader who projects enthusiasm and a sense of purpose can positively influence motivation, helping employees feel more connected to their work and their team.

Research in organizational psychology underscores the significance of emotional contagion in leadership, particularly in high-stress environments such as project management. When a leader demonstrates effective emotional regulation and consistently exhibits positive emotions, the ripple effect can enhance team cohesion, increase job satisfaction, and improve overall performance. This highlights the importance of leaders not only managing their own emotions but also recognizing the broader implications of how their emotional states affect others. Leaders who can harness emotional contagion strategically can create a culture of positivity, resilience, and collaboration.

Emotional contagion interacts with other psychological principles, such as social learning theory, which suggests that individuals model their behavior based on observing others. In the workplace, team members often look to their leaders for cues on how to react to challenges and stress. When a leader remains composed and solution-oriented, their behavior can serve as a model for how team members approach similar situations. This cause-and-effect dynamic reinforces the power of leadership in setting emotional norms within an organization.

Understanding emotional contagion also requires acknowledging its limitations and the potential for negative ripple effects. Leaders who are unaware of the emotional signals they send may unintentionally contribute to a toxic work environment. Negative emotions can reverberate through teams in ways that are subtle yet profoundly damaging, leading to increased stress, conflict, and disengagement. To avoid these negative reverberations, leaders must develop emotional intelligence—particularly in areas like self-awareness and self-regulation—to ensure that their emotional expressions align with the workplace climate they seek to create.

Moreover, emotional contagion is a powerful force in leadership, shaping the emotional landscape of teams and influencing organizational outcomes. Leaders who understand the ripple effect of their emotions can use this knowledge to foster a positive, cohesive workplace. Conversely, a failure to recognize the impact of emotional contagion can lead to negative reverberations that undermine team morale and productivity.

Try This: Actionable Steps for Enhancing Emotional Intelligence in Leadership

1. Practice Cognitive Restructuring

- **Exercise: Identify Negative Thoughts**: At the end of each day, jot down moments when negative thoughts about yourself or others surfaced at work. Reflect on the triggers and how these thoughts influenced your behavior.

- **Action: Examine the Evidence**: For each negative thought, write down evidence that supports and contradicts it. For example, if you thought, *"I always mess up presentations,"* list instances where you presented successfully.

- **Challenge and Reframe the Thought**: Replace negative thoughts with neutral or positive ones. For example, *"I *sometimes feel nervous during presentations, but I've prepared and can handle it."*

- **Test the New Thought**: Apply the reframed thought in your next similar situation and note the outcome. Over time, you'll build a habit of constructive self-talk.

2. Apply Emotional Regulation Techniques

- **Exercise: Emotion Labeling**: Throughout the day, pause to name the emotions you're experiencing. For example, *"I feel frustrated because my team missed a deadline."* Labeling emotions helps diffuse their intensity and increases self-awareness.

- **Action: Practice Deep Breathing**: When emotions feel overwhelming, use a simple breathing technique: inhale for 4 counts, hold for 4 counts, exhale for 4 counts, and pause for 4 counts. Repeat this cycle for a few minutes to regain composure.

- **Create a Personal "Reset" Plan**: Identify quick strategies to reset your emotional state when under pressure. This could include taking a short walk, listening to calming music, or doing a 5-minute mindfulness exercise.

3. Harness Emotional Contagion in Leadership

- **Exercise: Monitor Your Emotional Influence**: Observe how your emotions impact your team. For example, does your frustration lead to tension, or does your enthusiasm inspire motivation? Write down patterns you notice.

- **Action: Lead with Positive Energy**: Start meetings with an upbeat tone, express gratitude to team members, and share encouraging feedback. Positive emotions are contagious and can uplift team morale.

- **Recognize and Redirect Negative Contagion**: If you sense negativity spreading through your team, address it promptly. For instance, say, *"I sense there's some frustration about this project. Let's talk about what's causing it and how we can move forward."*

4. Integrate Emotional Regulation Theory into Decision-Making

- **Exercise: The Emotional Check-In**: Before making significant decisions, ask yourself: *"What emotions am I feeling about this decision? Are they influencing my judgment?"*

- **Action: Time Your Decisions Wisely**: Avoid making high-stakes decisions when emotions are heightened. Instead, schedule time to revisit the issue when you can approach it with a calm, balanced mindset.

- **Involve a Trusted Advisor**: When emotions are complex or overwhelming, discuss the situation with a colleague or mentor. A fresh perspective can help you balance emotions with logic.

Self-Assessment

Leadership Mindset and Emotional Intelligence

This self-assessment is designed to help you reflect on key aspects of emotional intelligence, project management mindset, and strategic leadership discussed in Chapters 1-3. Answer the questions honestly based on your current behaviors, attitudes, and practices. Use the scoring guide and interpretation below to evaluate your results and develop strategies for improvement.

Instructions:

Rate yourself on a scale of 1 to 5 for each statement:

1 = Strongly Disagree

2 = Disagree

3 = Neutral

4 = Agree

5 = Strongly Agree

Emotional Intelligence (EI)

1. I recognize and understand my emotions in various situations.
2. I stay calm and composed when faced with stressful or challenging scenarios.
3. I can empathize with others' perspectives and feelings, even when I disagree.
4. I handle interpersonal conflicts with sensitivity and professionalism.
5. I adjust my behavior based on the emotions and needs of others.

The Mindset of a Project Manager

1. I adapt quickly to changes and remain flexible in my thinking.

2. I identify and challenge cognitive biases in my decision-making process.

3. I manage stress effectively to avoid burnout and maintain focus.

4. I strike a balance between assertiveness and empathy when communicating.

5. I regularly monitor and address self-sabotaging behaviors.

Strategic Leadership and Psychological Forecasting

1. I proactively anticipate challenges and plan strategies to address them.

2. I use data and psychological insights to make informed decisions about team dynamics.

3. I foster a growth mindset within my team, encouraging development and learning.

4. I promote a collaborative environment to leverage diverse perspectives.

5. I evaluate team performance and adjust strategies to meet long-term goals.

Scoring and Interpretation:

1. Total your score for each section (Emotional Intelligence: Questions 1-5; Project Management Mindset: Questions 6-10; Strategic Leadership: Questions 11-15).

2. Refer to the interpretations below to understand your strengths and areas for growth.

Emotional Intelligence (EI):

- **21-25: Excellent!** You have a strong emotional intelligence foundation. Focus on refining specific skills like advanced empathy or conflict resolution.

- **16-20: Good.** But there's room for improvement. Practice active listening and work on regulating emotions during high-stress situations.

- **15 or below: EI needs attention.** Start with self-awareness exercises and practice emotional regulation techniques, like mindfulness or journaling.

Project Management Mindset:

- **21-25: Outstanding!** You demonstrate a balanced, adaptable, and self-aware approach to project management. Enhance your skills with advanced leadership courses.

- **16-20:** Solid progress. Improve by addressing cognitive biases and regularly reassessing how you handle stress.

- **15 or below:** Requires development. Work on self-regulation and resilience-building strategies, such as delegating tasks and setting boundaries.

Strategic Leadership:

- **21-25: Exceptional foresight and leadership ability.** Consider mentoring others or taking on roles that challenge your strategic vision.//
- **16-20: Developing well.** Focus on refining your predictive skills with psychometric tools or team performance analytics.
- **15 or below: Needs improvement.** Start by analyzing past leadership challenges and using those insights to plan better for future situations.

Strategies for Improvement:

Emotional Intelligence:

- Self-awareness: Journal daily to track emotional triggers and patterns.
- Empathy: Practice perspective-taking by actively asking team members about their experiences and emotions.
- Social Skills: Role-play difficult conversations to build confidence in resolving conflicts effectively.

Project Management Mindset:

- Cognitive flexibility: Solve puzzles or engage in activities that challenge your thinking, like brainstorming multiple solutions for a single problem.

- Stress Management: Integrate mindfulness practices, such as deep breathing exercises, into your daily routine.

- Avoiding biases: Before making a decision, list three alternative perspectives and evaluate their merits.

Strategic Leadership:

- Psychological forecasting: Use team surveys and analytics to predict challenges and gauge morale.

- Encouraging growth: Establish a reward system for innovation and learning among team members.

- Collaborative leadership: Schedule regular team brainstorming sessions to include diverse perspectives in problem-solving.

Case Study 1: Cognitive Restructuring in High-Stakes Leadership

Scenario:

Rebecca, a senior manager, is preparing to present a high-profile project update to the executive team. She finds herself overwhelmed by negative thoughts, including fears that her work will not meet expectations and that she may embarrass herself in front of senior leadership. These thoughts are beginning to impact her confidence and preparation for the presentation.

Questions:

1. What steps can Rebecca take to identify and challenge her negative thoughts using cognitive restructuring techniques?

2. How can examining the evidence help Rebecca gain a more realistic perspective on her concerns?

3. What role does testing new, positive thoughts play in helping Rebecca build her confidence for the presentation?

Case Study 2: Emotional Regulation During a Workplace Crisis

Scenario:

Jason, a team leader, receives unexpected news that a key client has decided to cancel their contract. The sudden announcement causes panic among his team members, who fear potential layoffs or project delays. Jason must manage his own emotional reaction while helping his team navigate the situation with clarity and composure.

Questions:

1. What emotional regulation strategies can Jason use to maintain composure and clarity during this crisis?

2. How can Jason's ability to regulate his emotions impact his team's response to the situation?

3. What steps can Jason take to help his team process their emotions and refocus on constructive solutions?

Case Study 3: Leveraging Emotional Contagion to Motivate a Team

Scenario:

Emma manages a marketing team tasked with developing a campaign for a high-stakes client. However, the team's morale is low due to tight deadlines and recent setbacks. Emma recognizes that her emotions and leadership style significantly influence her team's energy and motivation.

Questions:

1. How does emotional contagion play a role in Emma's ability to motivate her team during challenging times?

2. What specific actions can Emma take to ensure her positive emotions inspire and energize her team?

3. How can Emma balance emotional transparency with maintaining a professional and motivating demeanor?

Reflective Component

I encourage readers to:

- Reflect on how they have managed their own emotions or influenced others' emotions in similar scenarios.

- Write down three strategies they can use to improve their emotional regulation or cognitive restructuring skills.

- Consider how their emotional states and leadership styles contribute to team morale and overall workplace dynamics.

Chapter 4
Different Management Styles and Their Psychological Impact

Management styles play a pivotal role in shaping team dynamics, morale, and overall project success. Defined by a manager's approach to decision-making, communication, and leadership, these styles significantly influence how employees perceive their work environment and how effectively they perform. While no single style fits every situation, each has its psychological impact on team cohesion, motivation, and productivity.

Transactional Management

Transactional management is one of the most prevalent management styles, especially in traditional corporate environments where efficiency and structure are prioritized. It revolves around a system of rewards and penalties, with clear roles and responsibilities. This style is based on the idea that employees perform best when they know exactly what is expected of them and are incentivized to meet those expectations through tangible rewards such as bonuses, promotions, or public recognition. On the flip side, failure to meet these expectations can result in penalties like demotion, reduced bonuses, or reprimands. While effective in achieving short-term goals, this style is not without its limitations, especially when evaluated from a psychological and organizational development perspective.

At its core, transactional management taps into extrinsic motivation, where external rewards are the primary drivers of behavior. According to behavioral psychology, extrinsic motivation can lead to a strong focus on performance metrics, as employees are conditioned to meet specific objectives for immediate gains. However, this focus on external rewards often comes at the cost of intrinsic motivation—employees' internal desire to engage in a task for the sake of personal growth, satisfaction, or the joy of the work itself.

Transactional management can inadvertently create a psychologically limiting environment where employees feel confined to doing only what is required for the next reward. This type of conditional reinforcement can diminish creativity, as employees may become less willing to take risks or go beyond the scope of their defined roles. This happens because innovation and creative problem-solving often require intrinsic motivation, which is stifled when extrinsic rewards dominate the organizational culture.

In the modern workplace, transactional management might manifest in a setting where managers use structured performance evaluations and clear KPIs (key performance indicators) to gauge employee success. For example, in a sales-driven company, a transactional manager might set clear monthly targets for sales figures, and employees are rewarded with commissions and bonuses for meeting those targets. The focus is on measurable, short-term results—get the sales, hit the numbers, and you're rewarded.

However, the transactional approach also involves the risk of penalties for underperformance. In this sales example, employees who fail to meet their targets may lose out on bonuses or be subject to performance improvement plans. This transactional system, while motivating to some, can also induce stress and a narrow focus on individual success at the expense of teamwork and collaboration.

However, this type of environment is likely to produce mixed results. While some employees may thrive under clear, quantifiable objectives, others may feel stifled by the constant pressure to hit numbers and the lack of opportunities for creativity or growth beyond the immediate tasks at hand. Over time, this can foster an environment of complacency, where employees do just enough to meet expectations but lack engagement with the broader mission of the company. Transactional management can be effective for achieving short-term goals, especially in environments where tasks are routine and there is little need for innovation or creativity. In fact, transactional management excels in structured settings like manufacturing plants, customer service centers, or retail operations, where roles and tasks are clearly defined, and results can be measured quantitatively. It creates a sense of predictability and order, which can lead to efficiency.

This approach also has significant limitations, especially in environments that require adaptive thinking, innovation, or a strong sense of collective purpose. Employees under transactional leadership often focus solely on meeting baseline expectations to secure rewards, but this does not translate into long-term engagement or investment in the company's success. Over time, this can result in a workforce that feels disconnected from the company's vision, focusing instead on what they can gain in the short term rather than contributing to sustained success.

In the context of project management, for example, a transactional manager might successfully guide a team to meet project deadlines and milestones. However, if the project requires creative problem-solving or innovation, the rigid structure of rewards and penalties might prevent team members from going beyond their standard duties to explore new approaches. This can lead to a scenario where the team meets its deadlines but fails to deliver the most innovative or high-quality outcome.

Transactional management can also lead to stress and burnout. The constant pressure to perform for rewards or to avoid penalties can create a heightened sense of anxiety, particularly for employees who may not thrive in high-pressure environments. Additionally, by focusing primarily on individual performance, transactional managers can foster an environment of competition rather than collaboration. This undermines team cohesion, as employees may prioritize their own performance over the success of the group.

Further, the reliance on external rewards undermines employees' ability to build resilience and internal satisfaction. Research in organizational psychology suggests that employees who rely heavily on extrinsic rewards are more likely to experience reduced job satisfaction and burnout compared to those who are motivated by intrinsic factors. In transactional settings, employees may find themselves disengaged from their work once the reward is achieved, and without the intrinsic motivation to keep them invested, their long-term commitment to the company can falter.

Some would say that transactional management's over-reliance on extrinsic motivation, rigid structure, and narrow focus on immediate outcomes can result in disengagement, stifled creativity, and, ultimately, reduced long-term investment from employees. While this management style can be successful in structured environments, it requires careful balancing with opportunities for intrinsic motivation and personal growth to prevent complacency and burnout. In dynamic or innovative settings, a more flexible, transformational approach may be necessary to cultivate long-term success and employee satisfaction.

Laissez-faire Management

Laissez-faire management is a leadership style that takes a hands-off approach, granting employees autonomy over their work with minimal interference from the manager. The term "laissez-faire" is derived from a French phrase meaning "let do," emphasizing freedom and independence. In this management style, managers provide the necessary resources and tools for their employees but refrain from micromanaging or providing constant oversight. The responsibility for decision-making, task execution, and problem-solving is largely placed in the hands of the employees themselves.

While this approach can be highly effective in certain environments, especially those composed of highly skilled or creative teams, it can also lead to significant challenges, particularly in less experienced or less motivated groups. The psychological impact of laissez-faire management is varied: for some employees, it fosters independence and ownership over their work, but for others, it may generate confusion, anxiety, and a sense of being lost without clear guidance.

In a modern workplace, laissez-faire management might manifest in organizations that emphasize innovation, creativity, or technical expertise. For example, in a research and development team or a tech startup, a laissez-faire manager may trust their team to innovate and experiment without rigid guidelines. The team is free to pursue their ideas and manage their time, which can lead to breakthroughs and significant achievements. The manager may only intervene when necessary, such as providing resources or helping resolve complex issues, but otherwise maintains a distant supervisory role.

In these types of environments, laissez-faire management works because the employees are already self-driven, experienced, and intrinsically motivated. They thrive on autonomy and can navigate the challenges of their work independently. The lack of constant oversight allows them the space to think creatively, innovate, and explore new solutions without the constraints of a more rigid managerial structure.

However, in less skilled or less motivated teams, laissez-faire management can lead to problems. Without clear direction, employees may struggle to prioritize tasks, manage their time effectively, or collaborate efficiently. This can result in disorganization, low productivity, and even stress. Employees who are less self-motivated or lack the necessary experience may feel overwhelmed by the lack of support, leading to anxiety and frustration. In such cases, the laissez-faire approach can backfire, causing confusion and creating a vacuum of leadership that leaves the team without clear objectives or a sense of purpose.

Laissez-faire management can have both positive and negative effects, depending on the nature of the team and the individuals involved. For self-motivated and experienced employees, this approach can create a sense of empowerment and ownership over their work. The autonomy granted to them can enhance job satisfaction, as they feel trusted and valued by their manager. These employees tend to flourish in environments where they are given the freedom to explore their own ideas, make decisions, and drive their projects forward without unnecessary interference.

On the other hand, for employees who rely on more structure, guidance, and feedback, laissez-faire management can create a sense of abandonment. The lack of clear direction or involvement from the manager can cause confusion and uncertainty, leading to anxiety. Organizational psychology points out that employees need to understand their roles and expectations clearly, and the absence of this understanding can create stress and a sense of disconnection from the organization's broader goals.

All-in-all, in groups that require collaboration and cohesion, laissez-faire management can unintentionally foster silos, where individuals or subgroups work independently without proper communication or coordination. Without a strong guiding hand, team members may not align their efforts with the overall objectives of the project, leading to disjointed results and diminished productivity. This is particularly evident in teams that require clear, top-down communication to ensure consistency and cohesion.

This management style comes with significant risks, especially in more structured or hierarchical environments where clarity and guidance are essential. Inexperienced teams, or those in industries that rely on strict protocols and routines, may struggle under laissez-faire management, as the lack of supervision can lead to a drop in productivity, confusion about roles and responsibilities, and a sense of disorganization. Additionally, laissez-faire managers may fail to address problems as they arise, leading to unresolved conflicts, performance issues, or missed deadlines.

However, the effectiveness of laissez-faire management is heavily dependent on the context in which it is applied. In environments that demand creativity, independence, and a high level of expertise, this style can lead to outstanding results. Teams composed of highly skilled professionals who are confident in their abilities and intrinsically motivated can thrive under laissez-faire management, as it allows them the freedom to innovate and push boundaries without being constrained by managerial oversight.

A critical aspect of laissez-faire management is the psychological balance that managers must maintain. While the style emphasizes autonomy, the manager still has a responsibility to ensure that employees are not overwhelmed or directionless. Effective laissez-faire managers should be available when needed, offering guidance, resources, and support while still allowing employees the space to take ownership of their work. The psychological concept of "situational leadership" plays a key role here: the manager must adjust their involvement based on the needs and capabilities of the team.

In highly skilled teams, the manager may step back entirely, whereas in less experienced groups, a more hands-on approach may be necessary. Recognizing when to intervene and when to let employees operate autonomously is essential for striking the right balance in laissez-faire management.

Laissez-faire management is a mixed bag of potential benefits and risks, deeply dependent on the context in which it is applied. While it can foster independence, creativity, and job satisfaction in highly skilled and self-motivated teams, it may lead to anxiety, confusion, and low productivity in less experienced or directionless groups. The psychological impact of this management style is thus heavily influenced by the individuals and the team dynamics at play, requiring managers to be astute in assessing when and where to apply it effectively.

Authoritative Management

Authoritative management is a leadership style characterized by clear, decisive direction from the manager, who takes a firm but fair approach to guiding the team. It is based on the idea that a strong leader sets a defined vision, establishes clear expectations, and aligns the team toward achieving a shared goal. This approach often provides the team with structure, reducing uncertainty and increasing focus on objectives. However, while authoritative management is effective in many situations, its psychological impact can vary depending on how it is applied and received by the team.

Authoritative managers typically take the lead in decision-making, communicating their vision and setting specific goals that align with organizational priorities. This management style works best in environments that require strong leadership, such as in times of crisis change, or when a team needs direction due to inexperience or lack of confidence. The clarity that authoritative managers provide can be empowering for employees, offering a sense of stability and focus. However, when applied too rigidly, this approach can suppress individual initiative, causing employees to feel stifled and disengaged.

Authoritative management is distinct from authoritarian leadership, where control and compliance are imposed without room for flexibility. In authoritative management, the leader emphasizes a compelling vision and inspires others to follow it.

The manager typically provides direction, sets clear expectations, and encourages employees to contribute toward a shared goal. However, unlike authoritarian leaders who use coercion, authoritative managers use persuasion, logic, and motivation to get buy-in from their teams.

This style is highly effective when the team lacks direction or is faced with new challenges that require decisive action. The manager provides clarity, making decisions on behalf of the group and ensuring everyone understands their role in achieving the overall objective. In doing so, the authoritative leader instills a sense of purpose and alignment, helping teams stay on track and focused on long-term goals.

In today's workplace, authoritative management might be seen in environments that require decisive leadership, such as during organizational restructuring, project overhauls, or when a team is struggling with low productivity. For example, consider a product development team that has been unable to deliver results due to a lack of focus and conflicting priorities. An authoritative manager might step in, assess the situation, and redefine the project's vision, clearly communicating the steps required to bring the product to market.

The manager might set specific milestones, assign roles, and ensure that all team members understand their responsibilities. This provides much-needed structure, allowing the team to work more efficiently and with greater purpose. By offering this clear direction, the manager not only helps resolve confusion but also creates a sense of motivation within the team, who now understand how their work contributes to the overall success of the project.

Psychologically, authoritative management has a dual effect on employees, which can be both motivating and alienating, depending on the situation. In positive cases, it can foster a sense of security, as the team knows exactly what is expected of them and can align their efforts with the broader organizational vision. This clarity can reduce stress, enhance productivity, and give employees a sense of purpose, as they can see how their contributions directly impact the project's success.

Authoritative managers often have the ability to motivate teams through their confidence and decisiveness. Employees tend to perform better when they feel their leader is competent and knows the right direction to take. This sense of leadership instills trust and allows employees to focus on their tasks, knowing they have a capable leader to guide them.

However, the potential downside to this management style is that it can stifle creativity and innovation if applied too rigidly. Teams may feel constrained by the manager's dominance, as there may be little room for individual input or initiative. Over time, this can lead to a disengagement of employees who may feel their ideas are undervalued, creating a divide between leadership and staff. This is especially problematic in environments where adaptability and creativity are key to success.

Another risk is that authoritative managers can become overly directive, leading to a lack of team empowerment. Employees may feel that they are simply following orders rather than contributing meaningfully to the decision-making process. If feedback and collaboration are not actively encouraged, this approach can lead to a "command and control" dynamic, which may foster resentment or reduce morale over time.

One of the most important factors influencing the success of authoritative management is how the leader handles feedback. Effective authoritative managers understand that while they provide the overall direction, feedback from the team is crucial to ensure that the approach is working. By encouraging open communication and being receptive to suggestions or concerns, these managers can avoid the pitfalls of rigidity and build a stronger connection with their team. A manager who actively listens and adjusts their strategy based on team input can maintain the benefits of authoritative leadership while also fostering a sense of empowerment. This hybrid approach can prevent alienation and ensure that the team remains motivated, engaged, and invested in the long-term vision.

Overall, authoritative management is an effective leadership style in situations that demand clear direction, structure, and decisiveness. It provides a strong sense of focus and purpose, which can motivate employees and align their efforts toward shared goals. However, the psychological impact of this approach depends on how it is applied. If overused or applied without flexibility, authoritative management can suppress creativity and lead to disengagement. Successful authoritative leaders balance their decisiveness with openness to feedback, ensuring that their teams feel valued and empowered while working toward the collective goal of the team.

Servant Leadership

Servant leadership is a management style that prioritizes the needs, growth, and well-being of employees over the personal gain or power of the leader. Instead of commanding from a position of authority, servant leaders aim to serve their team by providing support, removing obstacles, and fostering an environment that allows employees to thrive. This approach emphasizes empathy, active listening, and a deep commitment to the personal and professional development of the team. Servant leadership is highly effective in creating trust, enhancing team cohesion, and fostering innovation, leading to long-term success for both the team and the organization.

The concept of servant leadership was first introduced by Robert K. Greenleaf in 1970 in his seminal essay The Servant as Leader. Greenleaf argued that the best leaders are those who focus on the needs of others and strive to help their team members grow and succeed. Since then, servant leadership has become increasingly popular, particularly as organizations place greater value on ethical leadership and employee well-being. This shift has been driven by a growing recognition that employees perform better when they feel valued and supported rather than simply being directed or controlled by a leader. This leadership style gained traction in modern society, particularly in the 21st century, as organizational cultures shifted toward prioritizing employee well-being, mental health, and ethical practices. In an age where social responsibility and leadership integrity are highly valued, servant leadership resonates as a powerful alternative to more traditional authoritarian styles. Companies such as Southwest Airlines and Starbucks have adopted servant leadership principles, recognizing that a focus on employee well-being leads to better customer service, increased innovation, and sustainable success.

Servant leadership can be defined as a philosophy or approach to management in which the leader prioritizes the well-being and development of their team members. The leader's role is to serve the team by empowering individuals, creating an environment of trust, and fostering growth both personally and professionally. In contrast to traditional leadership styles that emphasize authority and control, servant leaders lead by example, setting a tone of humility, empathy, and selflessness.

One key characteristic of servant leadership is the emphasis on building strong interpersonal relationships. Servant leaders focus on understanding the unique needs and motivations of each team member, and they actively work to meet those needs. This often involves providing mentorship, offering opportunities for development, and encouraging employees to take ownership of their work. By prioritizing the success and well-being of the team, servant leaders create an environment where employees feel valued, respected, and empowered to contribute meaningfully.

The psychological impact of servant leadership is profound, as it creates a sense of safety, trust, and belonging within the team. This feeling of security allows employees to take risks, be creative, and innovate without the fear of harsh judgment or failure. When employees feel supported by their leader, they are more likely to be engaged in their work, leading to higher levels of productivity, job satisfaction, and commitment to the organization.

Empathy, a core component of servant leadership, plays a crucial role in shaping this positive work environment. By actively listening to and understanding the emotions and concerns of their team members, servant leaders build trust and foster open communication. This, in turn, creates a culture of transparency where employees feel comfortable sharing their ideas, giving feedback, and addressing challenges. Such an environment is conducive to collaboration, teamwork, and long-term loyalty to both the leader and the organization.

Servant leadership promotes psychological empowerment by encouraging employees to take initiative and make decisions.

This autonomy can boost employees' confidence and sense of ownership over their work, leading to increased motivation and a stronger connection to the team's goals. Over time, this results in a more cohesive and high-performing team, as employees feel intrinsically motivated to contribute to the success of the organization.

In this way, rather than simply assigning tasks and expecting results, the project manager should spend time understanding each developer's strengths, weaknesses, and professional goals. The project manager should create opportunities for team members to take on leadership roles within smaller projects, mentor newer employees, and continuously ask for feedback on how they can improve their support. It is also important to implement regular one-on-one meetings, where employees are encouraged to discuss their career aspirations, any challenges they are facing, and personal development goals. By doing so, the manager can help their team members grow both professionally and personally, while fostering a sense of trust and loyalty. The servant leader focuses on the long-term success of their employees rather than short-term results. By building a team that feels supported, valued, and trusted, the project manager enhances team morale, increases retention rates, and encourages innovation, ultimately benefiting the entire organization.

Several frameworks exist to further define servant leadership. One popular model includes Laub's Organizational Leadership Assessment, which breaks down servant leadership into six key areas: values people, develops people, builds community, displays authenticity, provides leadership, and shares leadership. Another framework, The Spears Center for Servant-Leadership, identifies ten key principles, including listening, empathy, healing, awareness, persuasion, conceptualization, foresight, stewardship, commitment to the growth of people, and building community. These frameworks provide further depth to the concept of servant leadership and offer practical guidelines for leaders seeking to implement this approach.

Bureaucratic Management

Bureaucratic management is a highly structured and rule-based style that focuses on strict adherence to policies, regulations, and procedures. This style is most commonly found in organizations that prioritize consistency, compliance, and accuracy over innovation and creativity. In essence, bureaucratic management prioritizes a formal hierarchy and clearly defined roles, creating a system that relies heavily on protocols to guide decision-making and problem-solving. While this can ensure order and fairness in certain sectors like government or large corporations, it is largely ineffective in industries that require versatility, agility, or innovation.

Psychologically, bureaucratic management has significant effects on both individuals and teams. One of the primary concerns is that it can create an environment of rigidity, stifling creativity and autonomy. This is particularly detrimental in fast-paced or innovative industries where flexibility and out-of-the-box thinking are crucial. When employees are confined to stringent rules and processes, they are less likely to feel empowered to take initiative or think creatively. The sense of autonomy, which has been shown in psychological studies to be crucial for intrinsic motivation, is undermined in bureaucratic environments. As a result, employees often feel frustrated, disengaged, and demotivated, leading to decreased job satisfaction over time.

From a cognitive standpoint, bureaucratic management creates a narrow focus on rule-following rather than problem-solving, which can induce learned helplessness in employees. In situations where rigid processes fail to address unique challenges, employees may feel powerless to deviate from the prescribed methods. This learned helplessness can diminish both individual and team performance as the psychological barrier to innovative thinking becomes reinforced over time. Employees become conditioned to defer to the system rather than trust their own judgment, stifling growth and development.

The long-term implications of bureaucratic management are also concerning from a psychological perspective. Over time, employees in such environments may experience higher levels of burnout due to the lack of flexibility and the repetitive nature of their tasks. Research in organizational psychology indicates that employees who lack control over their work environment are more likely to experience stress and, ultimately, burnout. This can lead to higher turnover rates as employees seek more stimulating and empowering environments elsewhere. Additionally, when innovation and versatility are systematically suppressed, the organization risks becoming obsolete in competitive markets. The psychological stagnation of employees, coupled with organizational rigidity, prevents the firm from evolving with the changing demands of the industry.

In terms of interpersonal dynamics, bureaucratic management often fosters a climate of depersonalization. Because the focus is so heavily placed on processes and procedures, personal relationships and emotional intelligence tend to be deprioritized. This can damage team cohesion, trust, and morale. Employees may feel like mere cogs in the machine, contributing to a sense of alienation and disengagement from both their work and their colleagues.

An example of bureaucratic management in today's workplace might be a large government agency where every decision must pass through multiple levels of approval, and strict protocols dictate the execution of tasks. Even if a more efficient or innovative solution presents itself, employees may find themselves unable to implement it due to the rigid adherence to established procedures. While this guarantees compliance, it also guarantees stagnation.

In summary, bureaucratic management is most effective in highly regulated industries but is widely regarded as the least effective management style for industries where innovation, agility, and employee autonomy are key drivers of success. The psychological effects of this style—stifling creativity, reducing motivation, and increasing stress—can have long-lasting implications on both employee well-being and organizational success. When applied over the long term, bureaucratic management not only risks alienating its workforce but also jeopardizes the competitive edge of the organization.

Paternalistic Management

Paternalistic management is a leadership style where managers adopt a parental approach, making decisions on behalf of their employees while considering their well-being and personal development. Like a parent, the manager assumes a protective role, often deciding what they believe is in the team's best interest without necessarily consulting team members. This style encourages loyalty and commitment, as employees often feel cared for and protected by their leaders. However, paternalistic management can also come across as patronizing or condescending, which may stifle employee growth and independence.

In paternalistic management, the manager takes full responsibility for guiding the team, offering support, and ensuring the team has what it needs to succeed. While this can create a nurturing and stable work environment, the psychological impact on employees can be complex. On the one hand, employees may develop a strong sense of loyalty toward the manager, feeling appreciated and cared for. On the other hand, this style of management can create dependency, where employees become overly reliant on the manager for guidance and decision-making, thus inhibiting their personal growth and autonomy.

Psychologically, the effects of paternalistic management mirror those of a parent-child relationship, where employees may feel secure but lack the opportunity to develop their decision-making skills or take ownership of their work. This lack of autonomy can lead to stunted professional growth, as employees are not given the space to exercise their own judgment, take risks, or innovate. Over time, this can create a dynamic where employees are more focused on pleasing the manager or avoiding mistakes than on developing their own leadership skills or contributing creatively to the organization's success.

In today's workplace, paternalistic management is often seen in traditional or hierarchical organizations where there is a strong emphasis on respect for authority and loyalty to the leader. For instance, a manager in a family-owned business might adopt a paternalistic approach, making decisions for the team without consulting employees but with the aim of securing their well-being and maintaining a close-knit atmosphere. In such a setting, employees might feel grateful for the manager's protection and guidance but might also become less independent in their roles. This dynamic fosters loyalty but can limit creativity and long-term innovation.

An example of paternalistic management in practice could be seen in a mid-sized company where the manager decides to introduce a new workflow process. Instead of consulting the team for their input or ideas, the manager assumes they know what is best for the team based on their years of experience. The decision may improve efficiency and be well-received in the short term, but over time, employees may feel excluded from the decision-making process. This could result in employees viewing the manager as well-intentioned but overbearing, limiting their own sense of control and ownership over their work.

Paternalistic management can be moderately effective in environments where the manager's experience and expertise are highly valued. In industries that require a steady hand or in teams where employees are new and need guidance, this management style can help create a secure and stable foundation. For instance, in a healthcare setting, where new nurses or medical staff need to follow strict protocols, a paternalistic leader can provide the necessary structure and guidance to ensure the team functions effectively. However, in more creative or fast-paced industries, this style may be less effective as it does not encourage the independent thinking and rapid decision-making that is often required.

In the long term, paternalistic management can have mixed effects. While it can foster strong loyalty and trust, the lack of employee involvement in decision-making can lead to a passive workforce. Employees may struggle to develop leadership qualities or take initiative, relying on the manager for direction. This not only limits individual growth but can also hinder the team's overall potential to innovate and adapt to change.

In summary, paternalistic management offers a nurturing, protective approach that can foster strong loyalty and a sense of security within a team. However, its limitations lie in the potential to stifle autonomy and creativity, creating a dependency on the manager that may hinder long-term growth and innovation. While it can be effective in specific environments where stability and guidance are necessary, this style can be condescending if overused and may not work well in industries that require flexibility, agility, and employee initiative.

Micromanagement

Micromanagement is a management style characterized by excessive oversight and control of every aspect of an employee's work. Micromanagers often feel the need to direct every task, scrutinize every detail, and continuously monitor employees' performance, leaving little room for autonomy or independent decision-making. This style is widely regarded as one of the least effective because it stifles creativity, erodes trust, and contributes to a toxic work environment. While the intention behind micromanagement may be to ensure perfection and maintain control, it often has the opposite effect, leading to decreased productivity, low morale, and high turnover.

From a psychological perspective, micromanagement has profound implications for both cognitive and behavioral functioning within the workplace. Cognitive psychology, which deals with mental processes such as perception, memory, and problem-solving, suggests that employees under constant supervision are less likely to develop confidence in their own abilities. Micromanagement erodes self-efficacy—the belief in one's ability to succeed in specific situations or accomplish tasks—leading employees to doubt their skills and judgment. As a result, they may become overly reliant on their manager for approval and guidance, which undermines their ability to work independently or take initiative.

Behaviorally, micromanagement leads to a decrease in motivation, as employees often feel that their contributions are not valued or trusted. The constant pressure to conform to the manager's expectations creates a sense of learned helplessness, where employees may feel that no matter how hard they work or how well they perform, they cannot meet the manager's standards. This leads to disengagement, reduced effort, and, in many cases, resentment toward the manager. Over time, this style of management fosters a negative feedback loop in which the manager's controlling behavior leads to poor employee performance, which in turn justifies further micromanagement.

Industrial and organizational psychology, which focuses on the behavior of individuals in the workplace, highlights the long-term consequences of micromanagement. In environments where this management style is prevalent, employees tend to exhibit higher levels of stress and anxiety. The continuous scrutiny and lack of trust create a psychologically unsafe work environment where employees are afraid to make mistakes or express their ideas. This chronic stress can lead to burnout, a state of emotional and physical exhaustion caused by prolonged exposure to stressors. Burnout, in turn, results in decreased productivity, absenteeism, and higher turnover rates as employees seek to escape the toxic environment created by micromanagement.

In today's workplace, micromanagement is particularly damaging, given the increasing emphasis on flexibility, creativity, and innovation. An example of micromanagement in a modern office setting might involve a manager who constantly checks in on employees, demands frequent updates on even the smallest tasks, and insists on approving every detail of a project.

For instance, in a tech company working on a new software product, a micromanager might require developers to submit hourly progress reports, dictate how specific lines of code should be written, and review every feature in painstaking detail. This level of control not only slows down the project but also frustrates employees, who feel that their expertise is undervalued.

The psychological impact of such micromanagement can be devastating. Developers who might otherwise enjoy autonomy in their work and have the freedom to experiment with new solutions may start to resent their lack of independence. Over time, they may disengage from their work, leading to lower job satisfaction, decreased creativity, and a lack of ownership over the project's success. The company, in turn, suffers from decreased innovation, as employees are more focused on meeting the manager's rigid expectations than on thinking outside the box.

The long-term effects of micromanagement extend beyond immediate team dynamics. High turnover rates are a common consequence of micromanagement, as employees who feel stifled by excessive control are more likely to seek opportunities elsewhere. This constant cycle of hiring and training new employees increases operational costs and disrupts team cohesion. Additionally, the company's reputation may suffer, as word-of-mouth from former employees or online reviews may label the organization as a place where autonomy is not valued.

From a behavioral and cognitive perspective, it is clear that micromanagement hinders not only individual performance but also team dynamics and organizational success. Employees under constant supervision become risk-averse, focusing on avoiding mistakes rather than seeking out opportunities for growth or innovation. In the long term, this creates a culture of compliance rather than creativity, where employees are discouraged from thinking critically or proposing new ideas. Furthermore, the psychological toll of micromanagement—marked by anxiety, frustration, and disengagement—can lead to widespread dissatisfaction and a high rate of burnout.

Micromanagement is a highly ineffective leadership style that undermines employee autonomy, stifles creativity, and creates a toxic work environment. From a psychological standpoint, its impact on self-efficacy, motivation, and emotional well-being is overwhelmingly negative. While the intention behind micromanagement may be to ensure control and perfection, its long-term consequences include low morale, high turnover, and decreased productivity. As workplaces continue to evolve toward more flexible and innovative models, micromanagement stands out as one of the least effective approaches to leadership, particularly in industries that rely on creativity and collaboration.

Democratic Management

Democratic management is a highly effective leadership style that emphasizes shared decision-making and values the input and perspectives of all team members. In this approach, managers actively seek the opinions and ideas of their employees, fostering a sense of collaboration and mutual respect. Rather than making unilateral decisions, democratic managers encourage open communication and collective problem-solving, allowing the team to contribute to the direction of projects and initiatives. This participatory approach promotes a sense of ownership and accountability among employees, making them feel valued and invested in the outcomes of their work. Democratic management is often regarded as one of the most effective styles for team engagement, creativity, and morale.

This management style has a profound impact on the cognitive and emotional functioning of employees. The democratic management style enhances employees' sense of autonomy and self-efficacy—the belief in their own abilities to influence outcomes. When employees are given a voice in decision-making processes, they feel empowered and capable, which boosts their confidence and motivation. Cognitive psychology suggests that when individuals perceive themselves as having control over their work environment, they are more likely to engage in creative problem-solving and critical thinking. In a democratic workplace, employees are more likely to take initiative, propose new ideas, and experiment with innovative solutions, as they know their contributions will be considered and respected.

Behaviorally, democratic management encourages collaboration and active participation. Employees in democratic teams are more likely to engage in cooperative behaviors, such as sharing information, offering support, and working together toward common goals. This collaborative atmosphere fosters trust among team members and between employees and management. As trust grows, employees feel more comfortable taking risks, expressing their opinions, and challenging the status quo, which can lead to higher levels of innovation and productivity. Furthermore, by involving employees in decision-making, democratic managers create a sense of shared responsibility, which can lead to higher levels of accountability and commitment to the success of the team.

Democratic management can be particularly effective in environments that require creativity and innovation, such as technology, marketing, or design industries. For example, in a modern tech company developing a new software product, a democratic manager might hold regular team meetings where each developer, designer, and engineer is encouraged to share their ideas and suggestions for improving the product. The manager would actively listen to the input, facilitate discussion, and make decisions based on the collective insights of the team rather than imposing a top-down approach. This participatory process not only helps generate a variety of ideas but also ensures that the team feels a sense of ownership over the final product, which can enhance their motivation and satisfaction.

The psychological impact of democratic management is also evident in the way it reinforces collective efficacy—the belief that the group as a whole can achieve its goals. When employees feel that their contributions are valued and that they are part of a team that works together to solve problems and make decisions, their sense of team cohesion and morale increases. This collective efficacy can create a positive feedback loop, where increased trust and collaboration lead to better team performance, which in turn strengthens the team's belief in its ability to succeed.

Democratic management also has long-term benefits from an industrial-organizational psychology perspective. Studies have shown that workplaces that prioritize employee participation and engagement tend to have lower turnover rates, higher levels of job satisfaction, and better overall performance. Employees who feel that they are part of the decision-making process are more likely to remain loyal to the organization, as they feel valued and appreciated. In contrast, employees in more autocratic or micromanaged environments are more likely to experience disengagement and dissatisfaction, leading to higher turnover and lower productivity.

However, while democratic management is highly effective in many situations, it is not without its challenges. One potential drawback of this style is that decision-making can become slower, as managers must take the time to solicit and consider input from all team members. In situations where quick decisions are required, democratic management may not be the most efficient approach. Additionally, this style relies on a high level of trust and communication within the team, and it may not work as well in environments where employees are disengaged or lack the necessary expertise to contribute meaningfully to decision-making.

Democratic management is a highly effective leadership style that fosters collaboration, trust, and innovation. By involving employees in decision-making and valuing their input, democratic managers create an environment where employees feel empowered, motivated, and accountable. While it may not be suitable for all situations, the psychological benefits of this approach include enhanced autonomy, self-efficacy, and collective efficacy, all of which contribute to higher levels of job satisfaction and employee cohesion.

Transformational Management

Transformational management is widely regarded as the most effective leadership style for fostering team morale, long-term success, and innovation. It stands apart from other management approaches due to its focus on motivating and inspiring employees to exceed expectations and achieve their full potential. Unlike transactional management, which focuses on maintaining the status quo through rewards and punishments, transformational managers lead by creating a vision for the future, empowering their teams, and encouraging personal and professional growth. This style is considered highly effective for driving change, fostering innovation, and creating a positive organizational culture.

Transformational management is defined by its emphasis on motivation, vision, and employee development. At its core, it focuses on transforming both individuals and organizations by encouraging continuous improvement. Managers who adopt this approach are not content with simply maintaining operational efficiency; instead, they aim to inspire their teams to reach new levels of achievement. This style involves creating a shared vision for the future and helping employees see their role in achieving that vision. It is characterized by a deep commitment to developing team members, not just as workers but as individuals capable of growth and self-actualization.

In today's workplace, transformational management would look like a leader who constantly engages with their team, offering guidance, mentorship, and opportunities for development. For example, a transformational manager in a tech company might encourage their employees to take part in professional development workshops, collaborate on innovative projects, and participate in decision-making processes that shape the future of the organization. This manager would regularly communicate a clear vision of where the company is headed, making sure that each employee understands how their contributions directly impact that larger goal. In such an environment, employees feel empowered, valued, and motivated to take ownership of their work and to push their own boundaries.

From a cognitive and behavioral perspective, transformational management significantly impacts how employees think and behave. Cognitively, it enhances self-efficacy, which is the belief in one's ability to accomplish tasks and goals. When employees are empowered by their manager, they develop greater confidence in their skills and are more likely to take on challenging tasks with a proactive attitude. This sense of capability leads to increased intrinsic motivation—employees are driven by personal satisfaction and a desire for mastery rather than just external rewards. As a result, their job performance improves, and they are more willing to engage in creative problem-solving and innovation.

Behaviorally, transformational management fosters collaboration and engagement. Employees under this management style are more likely to engage in cooperative behaviors, such as sharing knowledge, supporting their colleagues, and working towards collective goals. This collaborative culture enhances team morale and cohesion, as employees feel that they are part of a supportive, growth-oriented environment. Additionally, transformational managers often use positive reinforcement to motivate their teams, recognizing achievements and providing constructive feedback that encourages continuous improvement.

The psychological impact of transformational management is overwhelmingly positive. Employees who are managed by transformational leaders tend to experience higher levels of job satisfaction, engagement, and commitment to the organization. One of the key reasons for this is the emotional connection that transformational managers build with their teams. By providing a sense of purpose and meaning in their work, transformational leaders create an environment where employees feel valued, respected, and appreciated. This fosters loyalty and reduces turnover, as employees are more likely to stay with an organization where they feel supported and have opportunities for growth.

The long-term implications of transformational management are profound. Teams led by transformational managers tend to perform better over time due to the strong sense of shared vision and collective goals. This management style promotes a culture of continuous learning and innovation, which drives sustainable success. Employees are encouraged to take risks, experiment with new ideas, and learn from their mistakes, all of which contribute to the organization's versatility and resilience through times of transition. In terms of industrial psychology, transformational management aligns closely with the principles of employee engagement and organizational development. Research has shown that engaged employees are more productive, more innovative, and less likely to leave their jobs. Transformational managers play a crucial role in creating the conditions for high employee engagement by fostering a sense of purpose, providing opportunities for development, and cultivating a positive work environment.

Transformational management is the most effective leadership style for creating a motivated, engaged, and high-performing team. By focusing on vision, motivation, and personal growth, transformational managers inspire their employees to achieve their full potential. The psychological effects of this management style—enhanced self-efficacy, increased job satisfaction, and stronger commitment—lead to long-term success for both individuals and organizations. In a transformational work environment, employees are not just doing their jobs; they are growing, learning, and contributing to something greater, which reverberates in both their professional and personal lives.

Narcissistic Management

Narcissistic management is a polarizing and controversial leadership style that, despite its negative connotations, can sometimes drive remarkable results. While often dismissed due to its association with egotism, manipulation, and a lack of empathy, narcissistic managers can be extraordinarily effective in the short term, leveraging their charisma, boldness, and relentless ambition to push teams toward success. However, this approach often comes at a significant psychological cost to both the manager and the team. Employees managed under this style can feel undervalued, and despite producing stellar results, they often suffer from high stress, burnout, and long-term resentment. This dual nature—high effectiveness with damaging consequences—makes narcissistic management a uniquely fascinating style worth exploring.

At its core, narcissistic management is characterized by self-centered leadership, a need for admiration, and a constant desire to be recognized as the best. Narcissistic managers are typically highly ambitious, charismatic, and willing to take significant risks. They believe strongly in their own abilities and often position themselves as the driving force behind their team's success. This can be incredibly motivating for employees, especially those who seek to gain the approval and recognition of a leader who seems larger-than-life. In fact, research shows that narcissistic traits are common among CEOs and other high-ranking executives because these individuals possess the boldness and self-confidence needed to navigate cutthroat corporate environments. This style has also been seen in political figures, with past presidents exhibiting these traits to command attention and rally followers.

The narcissistic management might look like a CEO or department head who thrives on control, recognition, and personal achievement. This manager could make grand speeches about the company's goals and vision, positioning themselves as the one indispensable figure capable of driving success. An example of this might be a tech startup CEO who relentlessly pushes their team to innovate, promising that their company is on the verge of revolutionizing the industry. While their speeches and vision are motivating, the CEO's need for personal validation drives them to place immense pressure on their employees, demanding constant proof of their loyalty, talent, and dedication. Under a narcissistic manager, employees often feel an intense need to prove themselves. Narcissistic managers frequently create environments where competition is not only encouraged but essential. Employees, wanting to gain the favor and recognition of their leader, push themselves to deliver exceptional results, leading to heightened performance and innovation. This kind of competitive atmosphere often results in stellar work quality. Employees continuously strive for perfection, knowing that their manager is hypercritical and has an insatiable appetite for success.

From a cognitive and behavioral perspective, this style plays into deep psychological needs for validation and recognition, both for the manager and the employees. For the narcissistic manager, leadership becomes a platform for fulfilling their need for admiration and control. They are motivated by the belief that they are superior to others and that their leadership is indispensable. For the employees, cognitive dissonance often plays a role. They may internally disagree with the narcissistic behavior but still, comply because they recognize that high performance leads to praise and professional advancement. Over time, this cognitive dissonance can create internal conflict, leading to stress and dissatisfaction. Behaviorally, narcissistic management can foster a toxic environment if left unchecked. Employees may become overly competitive, mistrustful, and even ruthless in their efforts to outshine their peers. While this can lead to short-term productivity spikes, the long-term consequences often include burnout, disengagement, and a breakdown in team cohesion. High turnover rates are common in environments led by narcissistic managers because employees eventually become exhausted by the constant pressure to perform and the lack of emotional support or empathy from their leader.

From an industrial psychology standpoint, narcissistic management can be seen as a double-edged sword. On one hand, the boldness and charisma of narcissistic leaders are often what drives organizational success, especially in industries where risk-taking and innovation are highly valued. These leaders are not afraid to make tough decisions or to challenge the status quo, which can lead to breakthroughs and rapid advancement. Many Fortune 500 CEOs exhibit narcissistic traits, using their larger-than-life personalities to steer their companies to new heights. However, industrial psychology also highlights the darker side of this management style—excessive self-focus and lack of empathy erode team morale, making it difficult for employees to stay engaged in the long run.

The psychological effects of narcissistic management on employees are profound. While the competitive environment created by the narcissistic manager can lead to high-quality work, it also fosters anxiety and fear of failure. Employees are often left feeling that no matter how hard they work, it's never quite good enough. The constant need for validation from the manager can lead to stress, feelings of inadequacy, and, over time, a decline in mental well-being. Even high performers, initially drawn to the challenge, may eventually feel emotionally drained and disillusioned. For the narcissistic manager, the psychological rewards are immediate—they thrive on the admiration and control they have over their team. However, in the long term, this management style can backfire. As employees grow tired of the lack of empathy and recognition for their contributions, they may begin to disengage or leave the organization altogether. This ultimately undermines the manager's success, as even the most charismatic leaders cannot sustain results without a motivated and cohesive team.

All in all, the narcissistic management style is a controversial yet highly effective leadership style, particularly in the short term. Narcissistic managers often deliver impressive results due to their charisma, risk-taking, and ability to inspire competition within their teams. However, this comes at a significant psychological cost to employees, who may experience anxiety, burnout, and long-term dissatisfaction. While some of the world's most successful CEOs and political figures have used this style to their advantage, its long-term effectiveness is questionable, as the psychological toll it takes on teams can lead to high turnover, disengagement, and a breakdown in trust.

The choice of management style plays a pivotal role in shaping both organizational effectiveness and the psychological well-being of employees. Positive management styles, such as transformational, servant, and democratic leadership, create environments that foster trust, collaboration, and personal development. From a psychological standpoint, these approaches enhance employee engagement and job satisfaction by emphasizing open communication, empathy, and shared goals. They empower individuals, promoting a sense of autonomy and collective efficacy that encourages creativity and long-term success. The resulting positive psychological impact can lead to increased motivation, lower turnover rates, and improved overall morale. Conversely, management styles that are more rigid or controlling—like micromanagement and bureaucratic management—often stifle innovation and create environments rife with stress and anxiety. Employees under such management may feel constrained, undervalued, or overly dependent on their supervisors. This can lead to disengagement and diminished productivity, as individuals may experience psychological fatigue and frustration in environments that do not support their needs for autonomy and growth. To effectively choose and identify a management style within a workplace, individuals should engage in self-reflection and observation. Understanding one's own values and leadership philosophies is the first step. Are you inclined to empower your team, or do you prefer to maintain control over every detail? Furthermore, assessing the psychological climate of the workplace is crucial. This can involve asking questions about how decisions are made—whether team input is sought, how conflicts are resolved, and how feedback is given.

Employees can identify their management style through direct communication with their supervisors, seeking clarity on leadership expectations and methods. They can also look for signs of the prevailing management style by observing team dynamics, the level of employee autonomy, and the overall morale of their colleagues. Understanding these elements can help individuals make informed decisions about the management styles that best align with their psychological needs and professional goals. Ultimately, the most effective management styles balance structure with flexibility, authority with empathy, and vision with collaboration. These approaches align organizational objectives with the psychological needs of the workforce, resulting in sustainable success and a healthier work environment. By recognizing the psychological implications of different management styles, leaders can better adapt their approaches to create an atmosphere that fosters both productivity and employee well-being.

Try This: Actionable Steps for Implementing Effective Management Styles

1. Identify and Adapt Your Default Style

- Exercise: Self-Assessment of Your Management Style

- Reflect on your current approach. Are you more directive, like an authoritative leader, or hands-off, like a laissez-faire manager? Write down three strengths and three challenges of your default style.

- Action: Seek Feedback from Your Team

- Ask your team for constructive feedback about your management style. Use questions like, *"What do you find most helpful about my leadership?"* and *"Are there areas where I could better support you?"*

- Adapt Based on Team Needs

- Match your style to the situation. For example, a transactional approach might work for routine tasks, but transformational leadership may inspire teams during change initiatives.

2. Balance Authority with Empathy

- Exercise: Empathy Mapping

- Choose a team member you lead and map out their perspective: What are their goals, challenges, and motivations? Use this insight to adapt your approach to their needs.

- Action: Empower Through Transparency

- Share the reasoning behind decisions and invite team input where appropriate. For example, in a democratic approach, say, *"Here's the challenge we're facing. I'd like to hear your thoughts before we finalize the plan."*

- Leverage Servant Leadership

- Regularly ask your team: *"What obstacles can I help you remove?"* Position yourself as a resource to support their success.

3. Mitigate the Downsides of Micromanagement

- Exercise: Delegate with Clarity

- Choose one task you typically oversee closely. Instead of micromanaging, delegate it with clear instructions and expectations, then step back and trust the process.

- Action: Practice the 80/20 Rule

- Focus your attention on the 20% of tasks that require your direct involvement while empowering your team to handle the remaining 80%.

- Establish Check-In Cadences

- Schedule regular, but not excessive, check-ins to monitor progress without stifling autonomy. For example, hold bi-weekly meetings instead of daily ones for ongoing projects.

4. Cultivate Transformational Leadership Skills

- Exercise: Vision-Crafting

- Write a clear and inspiring vision statement for your team or project. Share it with your team to foster alignment and excitement.

- Action: Celebrate Small Wins

- Acknowledge and celebrate progress toward long-term goals. For example, say, *"Your dedication to this project is making a real difference. Thank you for pushing us closer to our vision."*

- Empower Team Growth

- Encourage professional development by offering opportunities for skill-building, such as workshops, mentorships, or stretch assignments.

5. Recognize and Counter the Challenges of Narcissistic Leadership

- Exercise: Check Your Motivations

- Reflect on recent decisions you've made as a leader. Ask yourself: *"Was this decision made to benefit the team, or was it driven by personal validation?"*

- Action: Share Credit Openly

- Highlight the contributions of others during meetings and reports. For example, say, *"This success was made possible because of [specific team member's] efforts."*

- Prioritize Team-Wide Goals

- Shift focus from individual achievements to collective success. Regularly ask: *"How are we progressing as a team toward our shared objectives?"*

6. Promote Flexibility and Avoid Rigidity

- Exercise: Style Experimentation
- Over the next month, intentionally adopt a different management style for various scenarios. For instance, try a laissez-faire approach for creative brainstorming sessions and a bureaucratic style for compliance-heavy tasks.
- Action: Reflect on Results
- After each scenario, ask your team for feedback and evaluate the outcomes. Adjust your approach as needed to align with team dynamics and organizational goals.
- Blend Styles
- Recognize that successful leaders often blend elements of different management styles. For example, combine the vision of a transformational leader with the empathy of a servant leader.

Reflect and Recalibrate

Effective management is not about rigidly adhering to one style but about understanding the psychological impacts of different approaches and applying them thoughtfully. By practicing these exercises, you can foster a leadership style that aligns with your team's needs and evolves with changing circumstances.

Case Study 1: Balancing Transactional and Transformational Approaches

Scenario:

Ethan manages a sales team with aggressive quarterly targets. To ensure short-term performance, Ethan often relies on transactional management, offering bonuses for meeting targets and penalties for missing them. However, he notices that team morale is declining, and employees are less engaged in contributing innovative ideas. Ethan realizes he needs to incorporate elements of transformational management to inspire long-term growth and motivation.

Questions:

1. How can Ethan integrate transformational leadership principles while maintaining the structured benefits of transactional management?

2. What steps can Ethan take to improve team morale and foster a sense of purpose beyond short-term goals?

3. How might Ethan evaluate whether his leadership style is having a positive impact on the team's performance and engagement?

Case Study 2: Addressing the Risks of Micromanagement

Scenario:

Olivia, a project manager, is deeply involved in every aspect of her team's work, from minor tasks to major decisions. While she believes this ensures quality, her team members feel stifled and undervalued, leading to frustration and turnover. Olivia must confront her micromanagement tendencies and develop trust in her team's abilities.

Questions:

1. What psychological factors might be driving Olivia's micromanagement behavior, and how can she address them constructively?

2. How can Olivia rebuild trust and autonomy within her team while maintaining accountability?

3. What steps should Olivia take to transition to a more empowering leadership style, such as democratic or servant leadership?

Case Study 3: Managing a Narcissistic Leadership Style for Team Success

Scenario:

Liam, a department leader, exhibits traits of a narcissistic management style. He thrives on recognition and often positions himself as the driving force behind the team's successes. While his charisma and vision have led to short-term wins, his team feels overshadowed and underappreciated, leading to tension and declining motivation. Liam must find a way to temper his leadership style and create a more collaborative and inclusive team environment.

Questions:

1. How can Liam recognize and address the negative psychological impact of his leadership style on the team?

2. What steps can Liam take to ensure his leadership emphasizes team contributions and shared success?

3. How can Liam balance his need for recognition with fostering a collaborative and supportive workplace culture?

Reflective Component

I encourage you to:

- Reflect on their own management style and how it aligns with the needs of their team.

- Identify one specific behavior they can change or adopt to improve their leadership effectiveness.

- Write down three strategies for building a more adaptable leadership approach based on insights from these scenarios.

Chapter 5
Understanding Team Dynamics

Group formation and development is a critical aspect of understanding team dynamics, particularly in the workplace. A widely recognized framework that outlines the psychological stages of team growth is Tuckman's model, which breaks the process into five stages: forming, storming, norming, performing, and adjourning. This framework not only highlights the structural development of teams but also emphasizes the psychological and emotional transitions that team members undergo. Each stage represents a phase of evolving relationships, power dynamics, and communication patterns, all of which influence team productivity and cohesion.

The forming stage is marked by a sense of excitement and anticipation as team members come together with a shared purpose. Psychologically, this stage is characterized by uncertainty and cautious optimism. Team members are trying to establish their roles and boundaries, often leading to a high level of dependency on leadership. During this period, managers must provide clear direction and establish initial frameworks to guide behavior. Since the team is still forming, trust is not yet established, and individuals may hesitate to fully engage or voice their concerns. Leaders who adopt a supportive, guiding style can help ease the psychological tension that arises from ambiguity, ensuring that the team begins to align around common goals.

When the team begins to function more independently, it enters the storming phase. This stage is psychologically complex and often the most challenging for both the team and the leader. Conflicts may arise as individuals vie for roles, influence, and power within the group. Team members begin to test boundaries and push against the limits of the structure established during the forming phase. This can lead to frustration, anxiety, and interpersonal conflict. From a psychological standpoint, the storming phase can trigger stress responses as team members navigate these power struggles. However, it is also an essential stage for growth. Leaders must be adept at conflict resolution, using their authority to mediate tensions and realign the team's focus on shared objectives. Emotional intelligence becomes crucial in this stage, as managers must balance maintaining authority while fostering open communication to prevent long-term damage to relationships.

Following the storming phase, teams move into norming, where psychological stability begins to take hold. Team members develop a sense of cohesion and agreement around their roles and the team's processes. Norming is the stage where trust is more fully established, and individuals feel more secure in their roles and contributions. Psychologically, this stage fosters a sense of belonging and inclusion as team members start to appreciate each other's strengths and collaborate more effectively. For managers, this is an opportunity to promote shared leadership, delegate responsibilities, and empower individuals to take ownership of their tasks. The psychological shift from competition to cooperation is pivotal in this stage, as team members become more aligned with the group's collective goals rather than individual ambitions.

Once the team has fully established its norms, it moves into the performing stage, where high levels of productivity and efficiency are achieved. In this phase, the psychological aspects of teamwork are marked by confidence, mutual respect, and a high degree of autonomy. Team members trust one another and the leader, allowing them to operate with minimal supervision. The focus shifts from resolving interpersonal issues to achieving high-level goals and driving the organization's success. Leadership in this stage involves providing support and resources rather than micromanaging. The psychological satisfaction of contributing to a well-functioning team is at its peak during this stage, leading to enhanced motivation and overall job satisfaction. Teams operating in the performing stage are often resilient, able to adapt to challenges without major disruptions to performance.

The final stage, adjourning, reflects the psychological process of closure as the team disbands after achieving its objectives. This stage can bring a mix of emotions—pride for accomplishments, sadness at the dissolution of the group, and, in some cases, anxiety about future roles. Leaders must acknowledge the emotional complexity of this stage, offering recognition and support as team members transition to new roles or projects. The psychological impact of adjourning can influence how individuals approach future team dynamics, making it important for leaders to provide a sense of closure and celebrate the team's success.

Tuckman's model offers a clear framework for understanding team development from both a business and psychological perspective. Each stage of team growth is marked by shifts in power dynamics, emotional states, and trust levels, which require distinct leadership approaches. Managers who are attuned to the psychological factors influencing their teams can adapt their management style to fit the evolving needs of the group, ensuring both high performance and strong interpersonal relationship.

Role Definition and Role Conflict

Role definition and role conflict play a significant part in shaping team cohesion and overall performance in any organizational setting. From a psychological standpoint, the clarity of roles within a team can greatly influence how individuals perceive their work, interact with one another, and contribute to the collective effort. When roles are clearly defined, team members experience a sense of purpose and direction, which enhances collaboration, reduces misunderstandings, and ultimately supports the effectiveness of the team. However, role ambiguity and conflict can generate negative psychological effects that undermine team cohesion, leading to frustration, disengagement, and a reduction in productivity.

At the heart of effective team dynamics is the concept of role clarity. When each individual understands their responsibilities, expectations, and how their role fits into the broader team objectives, a psychological state of security and confidence emerges. People tend to perform better when they have a well-defined framework within which to operate. Psychologically, clear roles allow team members to focus their cognitive and emotional resources on accomplishing tasks rather than grappling with confusion or uncertainty. This clarity fosters a sense of personal accountability, where individuals know exactly how they can contribute to the team's success, creating a psychologically safe environment where collaboration flourishes. With reduced cognitive load and anxiety related to role uncertainty, individuals are more likely to engage proactively and support the team's collective goals.

Conversely, role ambiguity—a situation where roles are not clearly defined or communicated—has significant psychological consequences. When team members are unsure of their responsibilities or feel their roles overlap with others, stress and anxiety tend to increase. The psychological strain caused by role ambiguity manifests in various ways, including frustration, confusion, and even disengagement. This mental discomfort stems from a lack of direction, leading individuals to question their value within the team or organization. The cognitive dissonance between expectations and reality creates internal tension, making it difficult for team members to maintain focus, motivation, or a sense of accomplishment. Over time, persistent role ambiguity can erode team cohesion, as individuals may begin to disengage, feel demotivated, or even withdraw from their responsibilities entirely.

Another significant psychological disruptor to team cohesion is role conflict, which occurs when the expectations of a role are unclear, contradictory, or incompatible with other roles within the team. Role conflict introduces a significant degree of stress, as individuals may feel pulled in different directions by competing demands. Psychologically, role conflict heightens frustration, as team members may feel powerless to resolve the tension between conflicting duties. This constant tug-of-war between expectations can lead to emotional exhaustion, burnout, and dissatisfaction. Additionally, role conflict can erode trust within a team, as members may begin to question leadership's ability to manage and structure the group effectively. The mental toll of navigating conflicting roles can also result in strained interpersonal relationships, as individuals may misattribute their stress to the actions or inactions of their colleagues.

The long-term effects of role ambiguity and conflict are particularly damaging in high-stakes or fast-paced environments. When left unaddressed, these issues can cause a breakdown in communication, reduce morale, and impair overall team functionality. From a psychological perspective, prolonged exposure to these stressors diminishes individuals' sense of self-efficacy, making them less likely to take initiative or engage creatively in problem-solving. In some cases, role conflict can even escalate into open interpersonal conflict, further fragmenting the team and creating an environment of mistrust and resentment.

To mitigate these psychological stressors, effective role definition is crucial. Managers play an essential role in establishing and communicating clear responsibilities, ensuring that each team member understands their tasks and how they integrate into the larger organizational objectives. By proactively defining roles and addressing potential conflicts early, leaders can foster an environment where collaboration and mutual support are emphasized. A well-structured team, in which roles are transparent and coherent, allows individuals to direct their psychological resources toward achieving collective success rather than coping with the emotional burden of ambiguity and conflict.

Clear role definition is a fundamental aspect of maintaining team cohesion and optimizing performance. The psychological impact of ambiguous or conflicting roles is profound, affecting not only individual well-being but also the overall functionality of the team. Managers who take the time to clarify roles and responsibilities and who actively address potential conflicts can significantly reduce stress and frustration within the team. This leads to improved engagement, stronger relationships, and a more productive, harmonious work environment.

Psychological Safety and Trust

Psychological safety and trust form the bedrock of effective team collaboration and innovation. These intangible yet powerful elements enable team members to feel comfortable expressing their ideas, taking risks, and navigating conflict constructively. The creation of a psychologically safe environment is a critical aspect of leadership, as it directly influences how individuals engage with their work, their peers, and the organization as a whole. From a psychological standpoint, the presence or absence of psychological safety shapes not only the team's performance but also the long-term mental and emotional well-being of its members.

The concept of psychological safety refers to a shared belief among team members that the environment is conducive to open communication without fear of ridicule, punishment, or embarrassment. This sense of safety allows individuals to express their ideas, ask questions, and share concerns without worrying about negative repercussions. Individuals in psychologically safe environments are less likely to engage in self-censorship or defensive behavior, which liberates their creative and problem-solving capacities. The absence of psychological safety, on the other hand, can trigger stress responses, leading to disengagement, ultimately stifling collaboration and innovation.

Trust, closely intertwined with psychological safety, is the foundation upon which teams can collaborate effectively. Trust develops when individuals believe their colleagues will act in the team's best interest, be reliable, and demonstrate integrity in their actions. From a psychological lens, trust is an emotional investment that allows individuals to feel secure in being vulnerable—whether through sharing ideas or admitting mistakes. When trust is present, team members are more likely to engage in candid conversations, seek feedback, and navigate conflicts with a constructive mindset. However, when trust is lacking, individuals become more guarded, and communication tends to become superficial, inhibiting authentic collaboration.

A key psychological challenge in cultivating trust and psychological safety within a team is the "baggage" or psychological residue that individuals bring from previous job experiences. Each person carries with them a set of expectations, beliefs, and emotional responses shaped by their past work environments, leadership styles, and interpersonal dynamics. This accumulation of psychological history influences how team members perceive new environments, including their willingness to trust colleagues and leaders. If a person has experienced negative leadership, unresolved conflicts, or a lack of support in past roles, they may enter a new team with heightened skepticism and self-protective behaviors. This psychological baggage can impede the establishment of trust and psychological safety, making it critical for leaders to actively create an environment that invites openness and mitigates past insecurities.

The creation of a psychologically safe space involves more than simply encouraging open communication—it requires consistent, empathetic leadership. Managers who prioritize emotional intelligence and understand the psychological underpinnings of team dynamics are more equipped to foster environments where trust can flourish. This includes demonstrating empathy, validating emotions, and practicing transparency in decision-making. When individuals feel heard and valued, their psychological defenses lower, allowing for more meaningful participation and collaboration. Over time, this nurtures a positive feedback loop: as trust builds, psychological safety increases, and as psychological safety strengthens, individuals become more willing to contribute their full cognitive and emotional resources to the team.

However, creating psychological safety is not a one-time initiative; it requires ongoing effort and sensitivity to the unique psychological needs of the team. People's life and career experiences, including both successes and traumas, inevitably influence their behavior and perceptions in the workplace. For example, individuals who have faced professional rejection or criticism may struggle with fear of failure or performance anxiety, even in supportive environments. Leaders must remain attuned to these latent psychological barriers and create a culture of continuous encouragement and support. Open communication channels, regular check-ins, and an emphasis on learning from mistakes can help individuals overcome their fears and engage more fully with the team.

Psychologically safe environments also have a profound impact on innovation and problem-solving. In teams where safety and trust are prioritized, individuals feel empowered to take intellectual risks without fearing failure or judgment. This risk-taking behavior is essential for innovation, as it encourages experimentation and creativity. Conversely, in environments where psychological safety is compromised, individuals are less likely to voice unconventional ideas, limiting the team's ability to think outside the box. Furthermore, teams lacking psychological safety often default to groupthink, where conformity stifles diverse perspectives and critical thinking.

The absence of psychological safety also exacerbates conflict, as unresolved tension can lead to festering resentments and breakdowns in communication. Teams that trust each other and feel psychologically safe are better equipped to handle conflict constructively, viewing disagreements as opportunities for growth rather than threats. This capacity for healthy conflict resolution enhances team cohesion and reduces the long-term psychological stress associated with unresolved disputes.

Psychological safety and trust are indispensable for high-functioning teams. The psychological impact of feeling safe to express oneself, take risks, and engage with others in a professional and authentic way cannot be overstated. Leaders who understand the cognitive and emotional dimensions of psychological safety are more capable of creating environments that foster collaboration, innovation, and resilience.

Interpersonal Communication

Interpersonal communication influences everything from task completion to the overall health of interpersonal relationships. Both verbal and non-verbal communication shape how individuals understand, respond to, and engage with one another. In a team environment, communication goes beyond mere information exchange; it forms the basis for trust, mutual understanding, and collective efficacy. From a psychological standpoint, effective communication facilitates smoother interactions and boosts team morale, while poor communication can breed confusion, misunderstandings, and conflict.

Communication is a multifaceted process involving more than just the transmission of words. Verbal communication, including the tone, pitch, and speed at which words are spoken, can convey emotion, authority, or doubt. On the other hand, non-verbal communication, including body language, eye contact, facial expressions, and posture, carries significant weight in interpersonal dynamics. Cognitive psychology suggests that humans process these signals unconsciously, allowing them to interpret the intentions and emotions of others. When communication breaks down, it often stems from misaligned verbal and non-verbal cues or misinterpretation of these subtle signals.

Consider a situation where a manager, Sarah, is leading a team meeting to address a missed deadline. Her verbal message is calm and professional, yet her body language—crossed arms, lack of eye contact, and a stiff posture—signals frustration. The team, though hearing her words, picks up on her non-verbal cues and interprets them as a sign of disappointment or irritation. This incongruence between Sarah's verbal and non-verbal communication leads to heightened anxiety among team members, even though she intended to create a constructive environment for problem-solving. This illustrates how non-verbal cues can significantly impact how a message is perceived, often creating cognitive dissonance in the minds of the recipients.

From a behavioral psychology perspective, communication patterns can either reinforce or undermine desired behaviors within a team. When managers use positive reinforcement, such as praise or encouragement, they can foster an environment where team members feel validated and motivated. However, unclear or inconsistent communication can lead to ambiguity in role expectations and task assignments, resulting in frustration and disengagement. Individuals are wired to seek clarity and predictability, as these conditions reduce cognitive load and anxiety. In teams where communication is inconsistent or muddled, individuals expend unnecessary mental resources attempting to interpret or clarify messages, which can detract from their productivity and engagement.

The psychology of group dynamics plays a crucial role in determining the effectiveness of interpersonal communication within teams. Team members bring diverse communication styles influenced by their backgrounds, experiences, and personalities. For example, some individuals may rely more heavily on direct, assertive communication, while others may prefer a more passive or reflective approach. These differences can either enhance or disrupt team cohesion, depending on how they are managed. Social identity theory suggests that individuals naturally categorize themselves and others into in-groups and out-groups based on shared characteristics, including communication styles. When team members communicate in ways that align with their in-group norms, it can reinforce team unity. However, communication styles that deviate from these norms may be perceived as alienating, leading to misunderstandings or conflict.

Effective managers recognize the psychological intricacies of communication and adapt their styles to fit the needs of the team. For instance, a manager leading a highly creative team might adopt a more open-ended and collaborative communication approach, encouraging brainstorming and diverse perspectives. In contrast, a manager leading a team focused on compliance or precision may employ more structured, directive communication to ensure accuracy and alignment with set procedures. Understanding the psychological makeup of a team allows managers to tailor their communication styles to foster collaboration and reduce miscommunication, thereby enhancing team morale and efficiency.

Moreover, the psychological concept of active listening is central to effective communication. Active listening involves not only hearing the words being spoken but also fully engaging with the speaker's intent and emotional undertones. In teams, managers who practice active listening are better equipped to understand the underlying concerns or motivations of their team members. This helps to build trust, as individuals feel heard and understood, which is crucial for maintaining psychological safety. When communication is one-sided or dismissive, it can lead to feelings of alienation and disengagement, eroding the foundation of trust within the team.

Take Brian, for example, a junior employee who consistently felt that his contributions were overlooked during meetings. Despite verbal cues of acknowledgment from his manager, the lack of follow-up or meaningful engagement left him feeling undervalued. Over time, this disengagement grew into frustration and resentment, leading Mark to withdraw from team activities. His cognitive dissonance between the manager's verbal affirmations and the lack of behavioral reinforcement created a disjointed experience that ultimately diminished his motivation. This situation underscores the importance of aligning verbal communication with action to ensure that team members feel genuinely included and valued.

On the cognitive side, poor communication also places a significant mental burden on team members, particularly when they must interpret or infer meaning from unclear messages. This cognitive overload can lead to decision fatigue, mistakes, and reduced problem-solving capacity. When individuals are preoccupied with deciphering vague instructions or conflicting messages, their ability to focus on core tasks is compromised. Behavioral psychology suggests that clear, concise communication reduces uncertainty and allows individuals to allocate their cognitive resources more efficiently toward task completion and innovation. The cognitive and behavioral intricacies of communication highlight the importance of clarity, active listening, and alignment between words and actions, all of which are vital. Managers must be attuned to both the verbal and non-verbal dimensions of communication, understanding how these signals influence the team's cognitive and emotional states.

Managing Creative Conflict Through Collaboration

In the realm of teamwork, creative conflict emerges as a critical catalyst for innovation and progress. Unlike destructive conflict, which can fracture relationships and hinder productivity, creative conflict leverages diverse ideas, perspectives, and approaches to propel teams toward novel solutions. By navigating this dynamic effectively, leaders can cultivate an environment where differences are not merely tolerated but celebrated as essential components of creativity and collaboration. This idea delves into the psychological underpinnings of creative conflict, examining factors such as openness to new ideas, tolerance for ambiguity, and emotional resilience, which are paramount for harnessing the potential of differing viewpoints.

Creative conflict often arises in teams comprised of individuals with varied backgrounds, expertise, and thought processes. Take, for instance, a product development team at a technology company tasked with creating a cutting-edge application. The team, led by Sarah, includes individuals from design, engineering, and marketing. During one of their brainstorming sessions, a heated debate ensues between Michael, the lead engineer, and Anna, the design specialist. Michael advocates for a highly technical, feature-rich approach, while Anna emphasizes a user-friendly, minimalist design. As tensions rise, it becomes evident that their differing perspectives stem from distinct underlying values: Michael prioritizes functionality and performance, while Anna focuses on user experience and aesthetic appeal.

In this scenario, the potential for creative conflict is palpable. However, without effective management, this friction could devolve into frustration and disengagement, ultimately hindering the team's progress. Recognizing this risk, Sarah adopts a proactive approach by fostering an atmosphere of psychological safety where team members feel comfortable expressing their viewpoints without fear of judgment. She encourages open dialogue, prompting each member to elaborate on their perspectives and the reasoning behind them. This strategy exemplifies the importance of psychological factors, such as openness to new ideas and emotional resilience, in navigating creative conflict.

As the discussion unfolds, Sarah introduces the concept of "collaborative brainstorming," urging the team to view their differences as a source of strength rather than division. By reframing the conflict as an opportunity for exploration, she cultivates a mindset that embraces ambiguity and encourages collective problem-solving. In doing so, Sarah facilitates a deeper understanding of the underlying concerns driving each individual's stance, allowing the team to transcend surface-level disagreements. This approach not only enhances collaboration but also fosters a sense of collective efficacy, where team members feel empowered to contribute to the creative process.

The dynamics of creative conflict also highlight the significance of emotional intelligence in managing team interactions. Sarah's ability to empathize with both Michael and Anna enables her to mediate the conversation effectively. By acknowledging their concerns, she validates their feelings, reinforcing their commitment to the team's shared goals. This emotional resilience is vital, as it encourages team members to remain engaged and invested in the process, even when facing challenging discussions.

As the session progresses, the team gradually moves toward a synthesis of their ideas, resulting in a hybrid design that incorporates both technical functionality and user-centric aesthetics. This collaborative solution emerges not from a compromise but from a deeper understanding and integration of diverse perspectives. The final product not only meets the technical specifications but also resonates with the target audience, exemplifying how effectively managed creative conflict can lead to innovative outcomes.

However, it is crucial to recognize that mismanaged creative differences can stifle innovation and lead to disengagement. If Sarah had allowed the conflict to escalate without intervention, the team could have experienced a breakdown in communication, resulting in a toxic atmosphere where members felt undervalued and reluctant to share their ideas. This highlights the importance of leadership in recognizing the potential of creative conflict and guiding teams through the complexities of collaboration.

All in all, managing creative conflict through collaboration involves a nuanced understanding of the psychological factors at play within teams. By fostering an environment that prioritizes openness, emotional resilience, and constructive dialogue, leaders can harness the power of differing perspectives to drive innovation and strengthen team dynamics. Embracing creative conflict not only enhances collaboration but also empowers teams to navigate challenges with agility and creativity, ultimately paving the way for breakthrough thinking and lucrative outcomes.

Try This: Actionable Steps for Enhancing Team Dynamics

1. Clarify Roles and Reduce Role Conflict

- **Exercise: Role Mapping**: Create a role map for your team. Write down each member's primary responsibilities and their overlapping duties with others. Share this map in a team meeting to confirm alignment and clarify any misconceptions.

- **Action: Define Clear Boundaries**: Ensure everyone knows their responsibilities and how their role contributes to the larger goal. For example, say, *"Your role focuses on client communication, while [colleague's name] will handle technical support. Let's collaborate to ensure seamless transitions."*

- **Resolve Role Conflicts Promptly**: If overlaps arise, address them by redefining expectations. Facilitate discussions between team members to negotiate responsibilities and prevent resentment.

2. Build Psychological Safety and Trust

- **Exercise: Team Reflection Sessions**: Schedule regular team meetings to discuss challenges and successes openly. Start with a simple prompt like, *"What's one thing that's working well for you, and what's one area where you need support?"*

- **Action: Lead by Example**: Show vulnerability by admitting mistakes or sharing learning experiences. For example, say, *"I realize I could have communicated better about [specific project]. I'll work on being clearer moving forward."* This encourages others to do the same.

- **Celebrate Contributions**: Recognize individual and team efforts to foster trust and appreciation. A quick shout-out in a meeting or a thank-you email can strengthen morale.

3. Strengthen Interpersonal Communication

- **Exercise: Active Listening Practice**: Pair team members for a one-on-one conversation where each person must summarize what the other says before responding. Debrief as a team to share insights on how this improved understanding.

- **Action: Establish Communication Norms**: Agree on norms like no interruptions during meetings or using a shared platform for updates. For example, say, *"Let's make it a habit to respond to Slack messages within 24 hours to maintain momentum."*

- **Encourage Feedback Loops**: Implement regular feedback sessions, such as quick "start, stop, continue" check-ins, to ensure ongoing alignment and understanding.

4. Manage Creative Conflict Through Collaboration

- **Exercise: Conflict Role-Play**: Divide the team into pairs to role-play a conflict scenario. Assign one person the role of mediator, and debrief as a group to discuss effective conflict resolution strategies.

- **Action: Focus on Common Goals**: When disagreements arise, steer the conversation toward shared objectives. For example, say, *"We both want this project to succeed. How can we combine our ideas to achieve the best outcome?"*

- **Emphasize Collaboration Over Competition**: Foster a team culture where differing viewpoints are seen as opportunities for innovation rather than challenges to authority. Encourage phrases like, *"Let's explore that idea further,"* instead of dismissive responses.

5. Foster Long-Term Cohesion

- **Exercise: Team Strengths Workshop**: Organize a session where each team member identifies their strengths and how they complement the team's goals. Use this as a basis to align roles with individual capabilities.

- **Action: Rotate Leadership Opportunities**: Provide team members with opportunities to lead small projects or initiatives, which builds confidence and appreciation for diverse perspectives.

- **Measure Team Dynamics**: Regularly evaluate team health using tools like anonymous surveys. Ask questions such as, *"Do you feel your contributions are valued?"* and *"How comfortable are you sharing new ideas?"* Adjust team strategies based on the results.

Reflect and Act

Team dynamics are not static—they require constant attention, adjustment, and care. By actively engaging with these exercises, you can create an environment where individuals feel valued, roles are clear, communication is effective, and conflicts spark creativity rather than discord.

Self-Assessment

Management Styles and Team Dynamics

This self-assessment helps you reflect on your leadership approach and your ability to foster effective team dynamics. Answer the following questions honestly to evaluate your strengths and areas for growth. Use the interpretations and improvement strategies provided to enhance your skills.

Instructions

Rate yourself on a scale of 1 to 5 for each statement:

1 = Strongly Disagree

2 = Disagree

3 = Neutral

4 = Agree

5 = Strongly Agree

Different Management Styles

1. I adapt my management style based on the needs of the team and the project.

2. I understand the psychological impact of different management styles on team morale and performance.

3. I actively balance assertiveness and empathy in my leadership approach.

4. I empower my team by practicing transformational leadership techniques.

5. I recognize when my management style needs adjustment for better outcomes.

Understanding Team Dynamics

1. I ensure that each team member's role is clearly defined and understood.

2. I foster psychological safety within my team, encouraging open communication and collaboration.

3. I address conflicts constructively and use them as opportunities for growth.

4. I promote effective interpersonal communication to minimize misunderstandings within the team.

5. I actively facilitate collaboration during creative conflicts to drive innovation.

Scoring and Interpretation

1. Total your scores for each section:

    - *Different Management Styles*: Questions 1-5

    - *Understanding Team Dynamics*: Questions 6-10

2. Interpret your results using the ranges below:

Different Management Styles

- **21-25: Excellent adaptability and awareness of the psychological impacts of management styles.** Continue refining your approach by exploring advanced leadership techniques.

- **16-20: Solid understanding, but room for growth.** Focus on tailoring your management style to diverse scenarios and improving the balance between empathy and authority.

- **15 or below: Needs improvement.** Prioritize understanding the strengths and weaknesses of different styles and their psychological impacts on your team.

Understanding Team Dynamics

- **21-25: Outstanding ability to manage and nurture team cohesion.** Consider mentoring others or leading initiatives to improve organizational dynamics.

- **16-20: Good foundation.** Work on enhancing interpersonal communication and ensuring psychological safety is consistently maintained.

- **15 or below:** Requires focused effort. Begin by clarifying roles and fostering trust to build stronger team dynamics.

Strategies for Improvement

Different Management Styles

- **Enhance Adaptability:** Schedule regular self-reviews of your leadership effectiveness. Ask yourself: *"What's working? What needs to change?"*

- **Balance Empathy and Authority:** Practice using empathetic phrases during difficult conversations, such as *"I understand your perspective, and here's why we need to move in this direction."*

- **Embrace Transformational Leadership:** Regularly communicate a compelling vision for your team and encourage them to align their goals with this vision.

Understanding Team Dynamics

- **Clarify Roles:** Create and share detailed job descriptions and ensure team members understand their responsibilities and how they contribute to larger goals.

- **Foster Psychological Safety:** Lead by example by admitting mistakes and encouraging feedback. Promote an environment where team members feel comfortable sharing concerns without fear of reprisal.

- **Leverage Conflict for Growth:** When conflicts arise, guide the team toward focusing on solutions rather than blame. Use facilitation techniques to ensure all voices are heard.

Team Diagnostic Survey

Evaluating Team Dynamics

This diagnostic survey is designed to help readers evaluate their team's strengths and areas for improvement in three critical aspects of team dynamics: communication patterns, conflict resolution effectiveness, and overall cohesion. Use this tool to reflect on your team's current state and identify actionable strategies to enhance performance and collaboration.

Instructions

Rate your team's behavior for each statement on a scale of 1 to 5:

1 = Strongly Disagree

2 = Disagree

3 = Neutral

4 = Agree

5 = Strongly Agree

Section 1: Communication Patterns

1. Team members openly share ideas, feedback, and information without fear of judgment.
2. There is a consistent flow of information between team members, minimizing misunderstandings.
3. Meetings are productive and include opportunities for everyone to contribute.
4. Team members actively listen to one another during discussions.
5. Feedback is given constructively and received with an open mind.

Section 2: Conflict Resolution Effectiveness

1. Disagreements within the team are addressed promptly and constructively.
2. Team members feel comfortable voicing differing opinions without fear of negative repercussions.
3. The team focuses on problem-solving rather than assigning blame during conflicts.
4. A designated process for resolving conflicts is known and followed by team members.
5. Resolutions reached during conflicts are fair and accepted by all parties involved.

Section 3: Overall Cohesion

1. Team members share a clear understanding of the team's goals and objectives.
2. There is mutual respect among all team members, regardless of roles or seniority.
3. Team members support one another during challenging tasks or periods.
4. The team works collaboratively, leveraging each member's unique strengths.
5. Team morale is consistently positive, fostering a sense of belonging and purpose.

Scoring and Interpretation

Step 1: Calculate Section Scores

- Add up your ratings for each section (Communication Patterns: Questions 1-5; Conflict Resolution Effectiveness: Questions 6-10; Overall Cohesion: Questions 11-15).

Step 2: Interpret Your Results

Section Scores (Out of 25):

- **21-25: Excellent.** Your team demonstrates strong dynamics in this area. Focus on maintaining these strengths while addressing other sections as needed.

- **16-20: Good,** but there's room for growth. Identify specific behaviors or practices to improve in this area.

- **15 or Below: Needs attention.** Prioritize strategies to address gaps and enhance team dynamics in this area.

Strategies for Improvement

Communication Patterns

- Implement weekly check-ins to encourage open dialogue.
- Foster active listening by summarizing key points during discussions.
- Provide team-wide training on constructive feedback techniques.

Conflict Resolution Effectiveness

- Develop and share a conflict resolution process that all team members agree to follow.
- Encourage a culture of respect by reinforcing the value of diverse opinions.
- Use mediators or third-party facilitators for particularly challenging conflicts.

Overall Cohesion

- Regularly revisit team goals to ensure alignment and shared understanding.
- Create opportunities for team-building activities to strengthen relationships.
- Celebrate team successes to boost morale and reinforce collaboration.

Case Study 1: Clarifying Role Definitions to Resolve Role Conflict

Scenario:

Michael leads a team where two members, Sarah and James, have overlapping responsibilities in client communication and project reporting. This has led to confusion, missed deadlines, and occasional friction between the two. Michael realizes that the lack of clearly defined roles is creating tension and affecting the team's overall efficiency.

Questions:

1. How can Michael analyze and clarify the roles and responsibilities of Sarah and James to resolve this conflict?

2. What strategies can Michael use to ensure all team members have a clear understanding of their own and others' roles?

3. How can defining roles improve team cohesion and reduce future misunderstandings?

Case Study 2: Building Psychological Safety to Strengthen Team Collaboration

Scenario:

Maria manages a team working on a high-stakes project. During meetings, she notices that some team members hesitate to share their ideas or voice concerns, fearing judgment or repercussions. This lack of open communication is stifling creativity and hindering problem-solving. Maria must foster a sense of psychological safety to encourage participation.

Questions:

1. What steps can Maria take to create an environment where team members feel comfortable sharing their ideas and concerns?

2. How might Maria address past behaviors or cultural norms within the team that have discouraged openness?

3. What benefits can psychological safety bring to team dynamics and project outcomes?

Case Study 3: Facilitating Creative Conflict for Innovative Solutions

Scenario:

Emma's team is tasked with brainstorming ideas for a new product launch. While the team has generated several creative ideas, disagreements about the best approach have escalated into heated arguments. Emma sees the potential for these conflicts to lead to innovative outcomes but recognizes the need to manage the discussions constructively.

Questions:

1. How can Emma use facilitation techniques to guide the team's conflict toward productive collaboration?

2. What strategies can Emma implement to ensure that differing perspectives are valued and integrated into the final decision?

3. How might managing creative conflict effectively lead to stronger team relationships and more innovative solutions?

Reflective Component

I encourage you to:

- Reflect on challenges you've faced with role conflict, psychological safety, or creative conflict in your own teams.

- Identify three key actions you can take to improve team dynamics based on the lessons from these scenarios.

- Consider how fostering trust, clarifying roles, and embracing creative differences could transform your leadership approach.

Chapter 6
Handling Resistance and Change

Resistance to change can manifest in many ways, with passive resistance being a less vocal but equally impactful form. Passive resistance behaviors, such as procrastination, superficial compliance, or withdrawal, can subtly undermine change efforts. Psychologically, these behaviors may emerge from cognitive dissonance, where an individual's beliefs or routines conflict with new demands, leading to unconscious resistance. In this context, passive resistance can stem from a lack of trust, fear of the unknown, or unresolved concerns. By understanding these underlying cognitive and behavioral patterns, managers can better detect and address these forms of resistance. This practice explores how managers can re-engage disengaged team members by fostering genuine buy-in, employing empathetic techniques, and personalizing their approach to address individual sources of resistance.

Empathy-Driven Change Management

Team members bring unique motivations, experiences, and perspectives, which shape their responses to change. An empathetic approach to leadership is essential for effective change management, as it involves understanding these individual differences and adapting support accordingly. Empathy enables managers to identify each team member's emotional and cognitive responses to change, which can include anxiety, excitement, or skepticism. By actively listening and providing validation, managers can reduce psychological discomfort and encourage trust. Practical empathy-driven strategies may include adjusting communication styles, offering additional resources, and ensuring that team members feel heard and understood. This approach not only fosters psychological safety but also strengthens team cohesion and morale during transitions.

Navigating Power Dynamics and Authority Challenges During Change

When change affects established roles or decision-making authority, it can evoke resistance rooted in perceived shifts in power. The psychological response to a potential loss of control can result in defensive behaviors or pushback against new initiatives. To mitigate this, managers must navigate these power dynamics carefully, addressing fears of diminished autonomy while emphasizing inclusivity. Creating a supportive structure in which employees feel involved and valued can alleviate these concerns. Empowering team members to contribute ideas or participate in decision-making fosters a sense of ownership and control over the change process, easing the adjustment and reducing resistance. By recognizing and addressing the cognitive impact of authority changes, managers can sustain engagement and encourage buy-in.

Growth Opportunities in Resistance

Resistance often signals underlying needs or perspectives that, when addressed, can enhance team dynamics. Managers can reframe resistance as a valuable source of insight, using it to identify potential improvements in the change process. This approach, focused on constructive feedback, involves acknowledging concerns and fostering open dialogue. Actively listening to resistance allows managers to pinpoint areas where change efforts may need refinement or where additional support is necessary. By viewing resistance as a growth opportunity, managers can foster a collaborative atmosphere in which feedback is encouraged, ultimately strengthening the team's resilience and adaptability.

Sustaining Change and Reinforcing New Norms

Once new practices are in place, reinforcing behaviors is crucial to prevent a reversion to old habits. From a behavioral psychology standpoint, consistent positive reinforcement helps solidify change by encouraging desirable actions and mindsets. Behavioral reinforcement techniques, such as positive feedback, incentives, and consistent communication, support the internalization of new behaviors, making them feel familiar and sustainable. Regular check-ins, progress evaluations, and adaptability in response to feedback keep the change process dynamic and relevant. Managers should strive to maintain momentum by celebrating milestones, providing resources, and fostering a team environment where adaptation is rewarded, reinforcing the value of change and sustaining progress over the long term.

Each of these practices provides essential tools for project managers to understand and manage resistance from a psychological perspective. By addressing individual concerns with empathy, creating an inclusive environment, and viewing resistance as an opportunity for growth, managers can foster a supportive atmosphere where change is seen as an opportunity rather than an imposition. Through behavioral reinforcement, managers can also secure long-term commitment, ensuring that new norms take root and contribute to a thriving, adaptable team culture.

Self-Reflection and Emotional Intelligence in Change Leadership

In project management and leadership, emotional intelligence and self-reflection form the backbone of effective change management. However, self-reflection, the ability to honestly evaluate one's own behaviors, thoughts, and emotions, is often overlooked or suppressed. Managers who practice self-reflection bring a crucial level of awareness to their role, allowing them to understand and control their reactions to change, empathize with team members, and adjust their strategies to foster a productive and supportive environment. Without self-reflection, leaders are vulnerable to reactive behavior, diminished trust, and strained relationships, which create ripples that negatively impact the entire team. Self-reflection requires that a person look inward, often confronting insecurities, biases, and personal anxieties. Yet, for many individuals, this is a daunting task. The difficulty stems from both biological and psychological factors: self-reflection necessitates cognitive processes that can provoke discomfort, anxiety, and even guilt. For some, personal histories of perfectionism, criticism, or trauma can also make self-reflection particularly challenging, often blocking this capacity and leading to reactive and ego-driven behavior. By understanding and addressing these barriers, leaders can cultivate a heightened emotional intelligence, becoming better equipped to guide their teams through change.

The Foundation of Self-Reflection in Leadership

Self-reflection can be seen as the capacity to turn inward, taking stock of one's experiences, motivations, and emotions. It is tied closely to the psychological construct of metacognition, or "thinking about one's thinking," which is a fundamental tool for effective decision-making. Research has shown that metacognition improves cognitive flexibility, helping individuals to adjust to changing circumstances and consider multiple perspectives. In a leadership context, self-reflection nurtures empathy and emotional intelligence, allowing managers to view situations through their team members' eyes.

However, self-reflection is more than merely thinking about one's actions; it involves understanding and regulating one's own emotional responses. Daniel Goleman, a leading figure in emotional intelligence theory, identified self-awareness and self-regulation as two key components of emotional intelligence. Managers who can accurately gauge their emotions and recognize their triggers will handle conflicts and challenges with greater composure. For instance, a manager who regularly reflects on their emotional responses may recognize that a tendency to feel anxious when facing tight deadlines is based on previous experiences or unexamined perfectionistic standards rather than the demands of the current situation. Through this awareness, the manager can then employ healthier coping strategies to lead more effectively.

Why Self-Reflection Is Difficult for Some

Despite its advantages, self-reflection can be particularly challenging for some, with roots in personality, upbringing, and even neurological patterns. The process of self-reflection is cognitively taxing, involving both the prefrontal cortex and emotional regulation centers in the brain. For some people, particularly those who grew up in environments that lacked emotional validation or encouraged self-criticism, this reflective capacity may have been stunted. From a young age, individuals exposed to critical or punitive environments may internalize a fear of self-scrutiny, associating it with shame or guilt. In such cases, instead of self-reflecting to improve, these individuals might develop mechanisms of self-defense or avoidance, such as denial or externalizing blame. For example, a child who is consistently blamed or punished without constructive feedback may grow into an adult who subconsciously avoids self-reflection, seeing it as a painful or futile endeavor. This defense mechanism then becomes embedded, affecting relationships and professional performance, often until it is consciously addressed. Character formation also plays a role in this process. Erik Erikson's theory of psychosocial development emphasizes that individuals who fail to achieve certain developmental milestones, such as building trust or developing a secure sense of identity, may struggle with introspection and self-acceptance. This struggle can become a barrier to self-reflection, making it difficult for managers to examine their own behavior objectively and leading them to rely on ingrained coping mechanisms that shield them from uncomfortable truths.

The Domino Effect of Lacking Self-Reflection

When managers fail to self-reflect, they can become trapped in a cycle of reactive behavior, blaming external factors for their frustrations rather than examining their own role. This "victim mentality" stymies growth and creates a negative atmosphere in which accountability is absent. Instead of seeing challenges as opportunities for improvement, managers and employees alike may feel disempowered and disengaged.

In a workplace setting, a lack of self-reflection can lead to negative domino effects on team dynamics and morale. For instance, a manager who constantly externalizes blame may cultivate an environment where team members feel anxious or uncertain, fearing they will be unfairly held accountable for mistakes. Without an example of accountability and emotional regulation from leadership, employees may mirror this behavior, exacerbating conflict and eroding trust. In high-stakes projects, this erosion of trust is especially detrimental, as it prevents open communication, diminishes cooperation, and reduces resilience to stress. On the contrary, managers who practice self-reflection serve as role models for emotional maturity and constructive growth. Their willingness to own mistakes, seek feedback, and regulate emotional responses creates a culture of openness and mutual respect, where team members feel secure in addressing challenges collaboratively.

Spotting and Supporting Non-Self-Reflective Individuals

Recognizing non-self-reflective team members requires careful observation and empathetic listening. Such individuals may exhibit a pattern of blaming others, rarely taking ownership of mistakes, or displaying a rigid perspective on challenges. They might deflect constructive criticism, become defensive in feedback sessions, or avoid discussing their role in team issues. These behaviors often signal a reluctance to engage in self-reflection, stemming from either a lack of awareness or a deeper psychological aversion. Managers can help these individuals by gently guiding them toward a more reflective mindset. Using non-judgmental language, leaders can encourage self-reflective practices, such as asking open-ended questions or inviting the team members to share their perspectives on recent challenges. For instance, instead of saying, "You need to take responsibility," a manager might ask, "What do you think went well in this project, and what might you want to do differently next time?" This approach reframes self-reflection as a positive, growth-oriented process rather than a punitive one.

Coaching Techniques for Fostering Self-Reflection

Encouraging self-reflection involves both direct support and gradual mindset shifts. Managers can implement regular feedback sessions that focus on growth, framing these sessions as collaborative discussions rather than assessments. This technique fosters psychological safety, encouraging employees to explore their reactions and motivations without fear of judgment. Using mindfulness exercises, journaling prompts, or structured reflections after each project can also reinforce the habit of self-reflection, helping employees develop greater awareness of their emotions and behaviors over time.

For example, a manager may establish a "reflection round" after team meetings, where each member is invited to share what they learned, any challenges they faced, and ways they could improve. Over time, these exercises build familiarity with self-reflection, making it an integral part of the team culture.

Enhancing Emotional Intelligence Through Self-Reflection

Self-reflection is also a pathway to heightened emotional intelligence, helping managers recognize and regulate their own emotions to better support their team. Through self-reflection, managers can learn to identify their triggers, such as perfectionism, stress, or fear of failure, that may cause unproductive reactions during times of change. By becoming aware of these tendencies, leaders can actively manage their responses, setting a balanced tone that reduces anxiety for their team members.

Additionally, self-reflection allows managers to connect with their team on a deeper level, fostering empathy and mutual understanding. A self-reflective manager can more easily identify with team members' struggles, demonstrating a genuine concern for their well-being and creating an atmosphere where team members feel valued and supported. This empathy-driven approach not only strengthens team dynamics but also enhances resilience, enabling both managers and employees to navigate the complexities of change with greater confidence and cohesion.

In summary, self-reflection is a transformative tool for managers, one that bolsters emotional intelligence, enhances leadership capabilities and improves team morale. By understanding the psychological barriers to self-reflection, managers can recognize the importance of this practice and foster a culture of introspection within their team. Through self-reflection, leaders not only elevate their own performance but also cultivate a positive, resilient, and adaptable team that thrives in the face of change.

Creating Change Readiness

Approaching change from a psychological perspective can foster an atmosphere where team members feel not only prepared for the upcoming shift but also genuinely aligned with the goals of the change. By addressing the psychological needs of employees and building a solid foundation, leaders can prepare their teams to navigate the transition smoothly, embracing the process rather than resisting it. This requires a blend of strategic planning, behavioral insights, and empathy to create an environment conducive to growth and adaptability.

One of the primary strategies for fostering change readiness is setting positive expectations. When leaders communicate the vision for change as an opportunity for growth, advancement, and improvement, employees are more likely to view the transition as a beneficial development. Positive expectation-setting aligns closely with the psychological concept of *observational learning*, where individuals model their attitudes and behaviors based on what they observe from trusted leaders. Leaders who frame the change with enthusiasm and confidence instill these sentiments in their teams, creating a cycle of optimism and trust. This process is strengthened when employees observe successful leaders demonstrating resilience and adaptability, which in turn motivates them to adopt similar attitudes.

Framing change as an opportunity also plays into the concept of *social proof*, a psychological phenomenon where people look to others to determine the appropriate response in uncertain situations. When leaders present change as a path to personal and collective development, it encourages employees to adopt this perspective as well, especially when they see colleagues responding positively. This approach can reduce anxiety and replace it with a constructive mindset, wherein employees feel compelled to participate actively in the change process rather than remaining passive observers.

Another critical element in creating change readiness is cultivating a growth mindset across the team. A growth mindset, which emphasizes the potential for continuous improvement, fosters resilience and openness in the face of new challenges. By embedding this mindset in the organizational culture, leaders can help employees see change as an opportunity to learn and expand their skills. This psychological shift requires consistent reinforcement through communications that emphasize adaptability and praise efforts to try new approaches, regardless of immediate success. Such reinforcement helps teams embrace challenges with a sense of agency, reducing the likelihood of fear-based resistance.

Transparency is also fundamental to fostering change readiness. When leaders share relevant information about the change process, including the reasons behind it, potential benefits, and anticipated challenges, it helps reduce uncertainty—a major contributor to resistance. From a psychological standpoint, uncertainty can create cognitive dissonance, where individuals experience discomfort when their expectations don't align with reality. By providing clarity and openness, leaders mitigate this dissonance, helping employees feel secure and confident in their role within the change process. Furthermore, transparent communication can bolster trust, a cornerstone of effective collaboration and engagement in times of transition. In addition to direct communication, creating change readiness also involves encouraging *social conformity* toward new norms associated with the change. By reinforcing behaviors that align with the change, such as flexibility, proactivity, and a willingness to innovate, leaders can influence the social dynamics within the team. As employees see these behaviors being normalized and rewarded, they are more likely to adopt them, even if they were initially resistant to the change. This psychological strategy is subtle yet powerful, as it leverages the natural human inclination to align with group behaviors and expectations.

Creating change readiness involves a careful combination of setting positive expectations, framing change as an opportunity, cultivating a growth mindset, ensuring transparency, and encouraging social conformity toward supportive behaviors. Leaders who focus on these strategies can create an environment where employees feel psychologically prepared for the transition, fostering a culture that is adaptive, resilient, and open to growth.

Managing Defensive Behavior

Managing defensive behavior is essential for leaders aiming to maintain productive team dynamics, particularly when implementing change or guiding employees through transitions. Defensive responses—such as denial, rationalization, and avoidance—are often rooted in the discomfort people experience when they feel threatened or criticized. Recognizing these responses early can help managers foster a more supportive environment, reducing resistance and facilitating smoother collaboration.

Defensive behavior typically emerges when an individual perceives a threat to their self-image, security, or autonomy. This is especially true if a manager has a confrontational, accusatory, or poorly constructed feedback style. When managers give feedback that is overly critical or framed in a way that feels accusatory, employees may feel they are being mistreated or judged unfairly. This perception activates a psychological response where the employee may assume the stance of a "victim," viewing themselves as needing to protect their worth or value. Defensive behavior can, therefore, be a form of self-preservation rooted in a person's drive to protect their sense of competence and avoid feelings of shame, guilt, or inadequacy.

Employees exhibiting defensive behavior may use a variety of defense mechanisms, including denial, rationalization, and avoidance. *Denial* serves as a barrier to acknowledging difficult realities or changes, as the employee convinces themselves that the problem doesn't exist or won't affect them. *Rationalization* involves the creation of alternative explanations or justifications, which allows the individual to shield themselves from uncomfortable truths. *Avoidance*, another defense mechanism, occurs when employees evade situations or conversations that may force them to confront these uncomfortable realities. In the context of a team, these behaviors can hinder open communication, block constructive feedback, and prevent progress toward collective goals.

To address and ultimately reduce defensive behavior, managers need to focus on creating psychological safety and building trust. Trust is particularly critical in these situations because an employee who perceives a threat will be resistant to change or feedback unless they feel secure. Developing this trust is an incremental process that requires consistency, transparency, and empathy. For instance, an employee who has experienced negative feedback or perceived mistreatment will likely require reassurance that future interactions will be constructive rather than accusatory. This may involve the manager consciously adjusting their communication approach to emphasize respect, understanding, and support rather than judgment or blame.

Effective managers can utilize a few key strategies to foster trust and reduce defensiveness. First, adopting a more *neutral tone and stance* during feedback conversations helps to avoid triggering a defensive reaction. When feedback is delivered in a non-judgmental, objective manner, it is less likely to be perceived as a personal attack. Second, employing *active listening* signals to the employee that their perspective is valued and heard, which can help diffuse feelings of defensiveness. When a team member feels genuinely listened to, they are less likely to perceive feedback as criticism and more likely to consider it constructively.

Managers should also be mindful of *self-determination theory*, which underscores the human need for autonomy, competence, and relatedness. Employees who feel that their autonomy or competence is being undermined may experience heightened defensiveness. Managers can use this insight to offer choices or emphasize areas where the employee has autonomy, thereby helping them feel more in control of the situation. This approach can ease the defensiveness that may arise when an employee perceives that their decision-making power or skill set is being called into question.

Moreover, managers must be aware of *implicit biases* that might affect their own behavior, which can lead to inadvertent mistreatment or inequitable communication. When managers recognize their biases, they can work proactively to communicate in a way that does not activate defensive mechanisms in team members. Leaders who acknowledge and manage their biases contribute to a workplace that is both fairer and more conducive to open dialogue, helping employees feel respected and less inclined to defend their values or performance.

Managers should provide specific, actionable feedback that avoids ambiguous language. Ambiguity can lead to unnecessary speculation and fear, which only exacerbates defensive behavior. Instead of focusing on personality traits or broad criticisms, constructive feedback should focus on specific behaviors and their impact on team goals. This type of feedback is more actionable and allows employees to focus on improvement rather than personal defense. When employees feel that managers are respectful and non-judgmental, they are more likely to lower their defenses and approach change or feedback with an open mind. Defensive behavior, when not properly addressed, can create barriers to personal and professional growth.

Try This: Actionable Steps for Handling Resistance and Change

1. Build Empathy-Driven Change Management Practices

- **Exercise: Empathy Mapping for Stakeholders**: Create an empathy map for individuals or groups affected by a change. On a sheet of paper, divide it into sections labeled "Feel," "Think," "Say," and "Do." Write down what the stakeholder might experience in each category during the transition. Use this map to guide your communication and support strategies.

- **Action: Personalize Communication**: Tailor your messages to address concerns and motivations. For example, say, *"I understand this shift might feel overwhelming, but here's how it will benefit your workflow in the long run."*

- **Hold Open Forums**: Host Q&A sessions where team members can voice concerns and receive real-time feedback, fostering transparency and trust.

2. Navigate Power Dynamics During Change

- **Exercise: Authority Mapping**: Identify key influencers and decision-makers in the change process. Consider how their support or resistance could impact others.

- **Action: Build Coalitions**: Engage influential team members early in the process to champion the change. For example, say, *"Your experience and leadership would be invaluable in helping the team adjust to this transition."*

- **Leverage Respectful Communication**: Acknowledge authority while presenting your case. Use phrases like, *"With your guidance, we can ensure this change is successful."*

3. Turn Resistance into Growth Opportunities

- **Exercise: Resistance Debrief Sessions**: After a challenging meeting or resistance event, debrief with your team. Discuss what caused the tension and brainstorm ways to address concerns constructively.

- **Action: Reframe Resistance as Input**: Shift your mindset by viewing resistance as valuable feedback. For example, say, *"Your concerns highlight an area we need to clarify or improve. Let's explore it further."*

- **Encourage Collaborative Problem-Solving**: Involve resistant team members in creating solutions. Ask, *"What would make this transition easier for you?"*

4. Sustain Change with Behavioral Reinforcement

- **Exercise: Positive Reinforcement Tracker**: Create a tracker for recognizing team members who adapt to new norms. Acknowledge small wins publicly, such as, *"I noticed how you embraced the new software today—great job adapting so quickly!"*

- **Action: Anchor New Behaviors**: Introduce rituals to reinforce changes, such as daily check-ins or weekly progress updates. Make these part of the team's routine.

- **Monitor and Adjust**: Continuously assess the effectiveness of new norms and adjust as needed. For example, say, *"We've noticed this approach isn't as effective as we hoped. Let's tweak it together."*

5. Foster Self-Reflection and Emotional Intelligence in Change Leadership

- **Exercise: Leadership Journaling**: Dedicate 10 minutes daily to journaling about your leadership decisions and emotional responses. Reflect on what worked well, what didn't, and what you learned.

- **Action: Encourage Team Self-Reflection**: Incorporate self-reflection prompts in meetings. For example, ask, *"What's one thing you've learned about yourself during this change?"*

- **Model Emotional Intelligence**: Demonstrate calmness and understanding during difficult transitions. Use statements like, *"I understand this is a tough adjustment, but let's focus on how we can work through it together."*

6. Create Change Readiness and Manage Defensive Behaviors

- **Exercise: Scenario Role-Play**: Role-play scenarios where defensive behaviors may arise. Practice de-escalation techniques, such as active listening and reframing negative feedback.

- **Action: Normalize Change Discussions**: Regularly discuss potential changes even when none are imminent to build readiness. For example, say, *"Let's imagine how we'd adapt if we needed to switch to a new tool."*

- **Address Defensive Reactions with Empathy**: Respond to defensiveness with understanding, saying, *"I hear your concerns, and I'd like to explore them further to find a solution together."*

Reflect and Act

Handling resistance and managing change effectively is an ongoing process that requires patience, empathy, and strategic thinking. By implementing these exercises, you'll not only guide your team through transitions but also foster resilience and adaptability that will benefit the organization in the long run.

Case Study 1: Managing Resistance Through Empathy-Driven Change Management

Scenario:

Lisa, a project manager, has been tasked with implementing a new workflow system. While the system promises efficiency, several team members resist the change, citing concerns about increased workload and the time required to learn the new process. Lisa recognizes the importance of addressing these concerns empathetically to build trust and engagement.

Questions:

1. How can Lisa use empathy to understand the specific concerns and fears of her team members regarding the new workflow system?

2. What strategies can Lisa implement to address these concerns while fostering a sense of inclusion and ownership in the change process?

3. How might Lisa communicate the benefits of the new system in a way that resonates with her team's individual motivations and needs?

Case Study 2: Navigating Power Dynamics and Reinforcing New Norms

Scenario:

Ethan leads a team where a senior employee, Laura, is struggling to adapt to a new leadership hierarchy introduced during an organizational restructuring. Laura perceives the change as a threat to her influence, creating tension among the team. Ethan must navigate these power dynamics to ensure a smooth transition and reinforce the new organizational structure.

Questions:

1. What steps can Ethan take to address Laura's concerns while maintaining the integrity of the new leadership hierarchy?

2. How can Ethan foster an inclusive environment that minimizes power struggles and encourages team collaboration during this transition?

3. What techniques can Ethan use to reinforce the new norms and help the team adjust to the changes without further resistance?

Case Study 3: Encouraging Self-Reflection to Reduce Defensive Behavior

Scenario:

David, a department head, notices that one of his team members, Sarah, often becomes defensive when receiving feedback, frequently shifting blame or rationalizing mistakes. David realizes that Sarah's behavior may stem from a lack of self-awareness and the inability to engage in productive self-reflection.

Questions:

1. How can David identify the root causes of Sarah's defensive behavior and help her understand its impact on the team dynamic?

2. What coaching techniques can David use to encourage Sarah to engage in self-reflection and develop greater emotional intelligence?

3. How might fostering self-reflection in Sarah contribute to her growth and the team's overall performance?

Reflective Component

I encourage you to:

- Reflect on instances where you have faced resistance to change or defensive behavior in their teams.

- Write down three specific actions you can take to foster empathy, manage power dynamics, or encourage self-reflection in your leadership practices.

- Consider how applying these insights could transform resistance or conflict into opportunities for growth and collaboration.

Chapter 7
Cognitive Load and Time Management

Cognitive load theory, first developed to address educational strategies, has since been applied to numerous fields, including project management. It reveals how mental strain impacts clarity of thought and decision quality, underscoring the importance of designing tasks and processes in a way that minimizes unnecessary mental burdens on team members. Cognitive load is multifaceted, composed of intrinsic, extraneous, and germane types, each of which impacts how individuals absorb, process, and respond to information. By recognizing these categories, managers can adopt strategies that optimize productivity, support mental clarity, and preserve cognitive resources for high-priority tasks.

Intrinsic cognitive load represents the inherent difficulty of a particular task. It is determined by the complexity of information that an individual needs to process, making it an unavoidable component of work. For example, learning a new project management software or analyzing complex data sets can place high intrinsic cognitive demands on team members. In cases of elevated intrinsic load, team members might feel overwhelmed, particularly when tasks require specialized knowledge or intense concentration. While intrinsic load cannot be entirely eliminated, it can be managed by appropriately distributing responsibilities across team members who possess the necessary skills or training. Training sessions, task breakdowns, and scaffolding can reduce intrinsic cognitive load, allowing team members to manage complex tasks without reaching cognitive exhaustion.

Extraneous cognitive load, on the other hand, involves mental strain created by unnecessary, inefficient, or poorly organized information. In the workplace, extraneous load often arises from unclear instructions, disorganized resources, redundant meetings, or excessive multitasking requirements. Unnecessary complexity distracts team members from focusing on core tasks and draws their mental resources toward navigating clutter rather than solving key problems. To reduce extraneous cognitive load, managers should prioritize concise and clear communication, streamline processes, and eliminate non-essential steps. Information architecture, such as how data is stored and accessed, also plays a role in minimizing extraneous load. When workspaces and digital resources are intuitively organized, team members spend less time searching for information, freeing mental energy to focus on priority tasks.

Germane cognitive load refers to the mental effort required to create meaningful understanding and to integrate new information with existing knowledge. Germane load can be positive when managed correctly, as it allows team members to deepen their expertise and build cognitive structures that facilitate better decision-making. In project management, promoting germane load may involve encouraging analytical thinking, problem-solving, and reflective discussions within teams. Managers should be aware of how much germane load team members can handle at a given time and encourage activities that foster meaningful learning rather than overwhelming them with excessive information. Balancing germane load is essential for maintaining a productive team environment where learning is supported without creating additional mental strain.

Understanding the relationship between cognitive load and productivity requires acknowledging that each load type competes for limited cognitive resources. When mental resources are overextended, decision quality declines, and team members are more likely to make errors or experience fatigue. Prolonged cognitive overload also increases the likelihood of stress-related symptoms, leading to mental strain that affects both professional and personal lives. Modern workplaces are often fast-paced and complex, with constant access to information and frequent interruptions, both of which compound mental strain. Moreover, external life stressors—such as personal challenges or family obligations—add to cognitive load and can affect one's resilience to workplace demands. Managers who recognize these additional burdens can better design tasks and set expectations that account for each team member's total mental load, ensuring work remains sustainable.

To mitigate the risk of cognitive overload, managers should take a proactive role in structuring work that respects cognitive limits. Task prioritization, chunking information, and pacing are effective strategies for preserving mental resources. Delegating appropriately and respecting the cognitive load levels that each team member can reasonably handle are vital practices. Open communication, regular feedback, and supportive team structures are also essential for managing cognitive load. Creating an environment where team members feel comfortable sharing feedback allows managers to gauge cognitive strain levels and adjust workflows accordingly. Cognitive load management is as much about fostering a sustainable, balanced work environment as it is about optimizing productivity.

The Mental Cost of Multitasking

Multitasking has long been perceived as a marker of efficiency, especially in high-stakes business environments where productivity and speed are often prioritized. However, the concept of multitasking as an effective productivity tool is largely a myth, and its negative impact on cognitive functioning is widely supported by research. Rather than improving productivity, multitasking divides attention and increases cognitive load, leading to poorer performance across tasks. This division of mental resources compromises memory retention, disrupts emotional resilience, and limits mental clarity, making it clear that the mental costs of multitasking outweigh any perceived benefits. A better understanding of the mechanisms behind multitasking's inefficacies reveals why businesses and leaders should shift their focus to time management strategies that respect cognitive limits and foster sustained, focused attention.

Central to understanding the limitations of multitasking is the concept of "task-switching cost." Task-switching cost is the cognitive and time-related penalty incurred when the brain repeatedly shifts focus from one task to another. While the brain is capable of task-switching, it is far less efficient than most assume. Each switch requires the brain to reorient itself to a new set of rules, goals, and stimuli, which consumes both mental energy and time. For even the simplest of tasks, these mental shifts lead to a measurable decline in performance and an increase in the likelihood of errors. Repeated task-switching also creates strain on working memory, leading to slower recall and increased forgetting. Thus, while multitasking may appear to expedite completion times, it ultimately reduces the quality and accuracy of work, making the practice counterproductive in professional settings.

Multitasking also has a significant impact on mental clarity and decision-making. Attempting to manage several tasks at once disperses cognitive resources across competing demands, making it difficult for individuals to engage in the deeper, sustained thought required for high-quality decision-making. Cognitive overload, brought on by excessive multitasking, impairs the ability to weigh options, anticipate outcomes, and analyze information comprehensively. The fragmented focus that results from multitasking not only hinders the accuracy of decisions but also limits the individual's ability to understand complex systems and relationships within their work. For leaders and managers, maintaining mental clarity is essential, as strategic planning and effective oversight depend on focused, deliberate thought. The myth of multitasking undermines these critical functions, making it a practice that contradicts the principles of effective leadership.

Memory retention is another casualty of multitasking. Memory, particularly short-term or working memory, is essential for efficient task performance. When individuals engage in multiple tasks simultaneously, the demands on working memory increase significantly, diminishing their ability to hold and retrieve information as needed. Continuous interruptions further compromise memory consolidation, as the brain cannot process and store information effectively while constantly switching contexts. Over time, this decline in memory performance affects productivity, as team members are forced to relearn information or repeat actions they may otherwise have retained. In a business context, where timely access to relevant knowledge is critical, multitasking leads to inefficient outcomes, wasted time, and redundant efforts—all of which diminish productivity.

Emotional resilience, an often overlooked aspect of cognitive performance, is also negatively impacted by multitasking. The continuous demand for rapid task-switching heightens stress and mental fatigue as the brain attempts to manage multiple streams of stimuli and information. This heightened state of cognitive arousal activates the brain's stress response, increasing cortisol levels and, over time, reducing resilience to stressors. For professionals, this decrease in emotional resilience can manifest as burnout, irritability, and a reduced capacity to handle workplace challenges with patience and composure. Resilience is an asset in high-demand environments, as it supports a positive mindset and long-term engagement. Multitasking, however, diminishes this asset, leaving individuals more susceptible to stress and more likely to experience negative emotional reactions.

Modern business practices increasingly recognize the drawbacks of multitasking and encourage time management strategies that prioritize focus over fragmentation. Implementing these strategies in professional environments means structuring tasks and workflows to align with the brain's natural preference for sustained attention. Practices such as "time-blocking," where specific blocks of time are dedicated to particular tasks, create an environment where employees can engage fully with one task without the disruption of constant task-switching. Time-blocking also respects the brain's limitations, preventing cognitive overload and promoting higher-quality work. Likewise, reducing unnecessary interruptions, such as redundant meetings and excessive emails, helps preserve mental energy and focus. These strategies align with the latest cognitive research, which advocates for reducing extraneous cognitive load to enhance productivity and mental well-being.

Additionally, promoting a culture of single-tasking over multitasking reinforces the value of focused work. Leaders who model this behavior can shift team dynamics, encouraging employees to prioritize tasks rather than attempt to juggle multiple responsibilities simultaneously. Emphasizing single-tasking as a core value helps to dispel the productivity myth associated with multitasking, fostering a more thoughtful and deliberate approach to work. In today's information-rich environments, where the demands for attention and cognitive processing continue to grow, acknowledging the mental cost of multitasking is essential for sustainable productivity.

The cognitive penalties of multitasking underscore the importance of time management skills as a buffer against mental strain. A well-organized approach to task completion helps maintain cognitive resources, supporting memory, decision-making, and emotional resilience. Managers who emphasize time management within their teams help mitigate the mental costs associated with multitasking, contributing to a work environment where cognitive clarity, effective decision-making, and sustained productivity are valued. Dispelling the myth of multitasking not only enhances performance but also promotes a healthier, more resilient workforce capable of meeting the demands of modern business environments without compromising mental well-being.

Prioritization Techniques to Reduce Cognitive Overload

With an influx of demands, responsibilities, and time-sensitive projects, effective prioritization techniques provide managers and their teams with the tools needed to maintain productivity without succumbing to cognitive fatigue. One of the primary advantages of structured prioritization is its role in preserving mental focus, which allows for better decision-making and clearer strategic thinking. When tasks are organized based on urgency and importance, individuals can concentrate on meaningful work while minimizing distractions, leading to more consistent outcomes and reduced cognitive strain.

A foundational technique for prioritization is the Eisenhower Matrix, a decision-making framework that categorizes tasks into four quadrants based on urgency and importance. By distinguishing between tasks that are both urgent and important versus those that are neither, managers can allocate their mental energy toward activities that drive long-term goals rather than short-term distractions. This method not only reduces unnecessary cognitive load but also enhances executive function, a set of cognitive processes that facilitate planning, attention, and goal achievement. The Eisenhower Matrix enables managers to make conscious, deliberate choices about task engagement, thereby protecting their cognitive resources from depletion and improving their capacity to manage complex workloads. It also fosters a sense of control and autonomy, which are crucial for maintaining cognitive resilience under pressure.

Task batching is another powerful strategy for reducing cognitive overload and maximizing productivity. By grouping similar tasks together, managers and team members can streamline mental processes, reducing the need for constant task-switching, which has been shown to disrupt cognitive flow and lead to "task-switching costs." When tasks of a similar nature are performed consecutively, the brain engages in repetitive action patterns, which reduces the amount of cognitive energy required to shift between different types of activities. This consolidation of mental resources aids in reducing extraneous cognitive load, enabling individuals to remain focused, efficient, and less prone to errors. Task batching is particularly effective in environments where rapid task-switching would otherwise lead to fragmentation of attention, ultimately minimizing the likelihood of burnout by maintaining a consistent cognitive rhythm.

Time-blocking, a technique in which specific time slots are designated for focused work on distinct tasks or projects, is equally effective in managing cognitive load. By scheduling uninterrupted time blocks for priority tasks, managers create an environment that minimizes distractions and encourages deep work, which refers to the state of sustained focus required for complex problem-solving and creative thinking. Time-blocking not only shields the brain from competing stimuli but also promotes the psychological concept of "flow," a state in which individuals are fully absorbed in their work and lose a sense of time. Engaging in flow states has been shown to improve task satisfaction and cognitive endurance, providing a sustainable framework for managing high-stakes projects while reducing cognitive fatigue. Furthermore, time-blocking allows for regular breaks between focused work intervals, giving the brain necessary recovery time to prevent mental exhaustion.

Effective prioritization also involves differentiating between urgent and important tasks, which helps managers avoid the common pitfall of treating all tasks as equally critical. Urgency often elicits a strong emotional response, leading to reactive decision-making that consumes cognitive resources and limits the ability to engage in reflective, strategic thinking. By training the mind to separate urgency from importance, managers build resilience against cognitive overload, creating a mental buffer that allows them to approach problems with greater clarity and control. Prioritizing based on importance enables individuals to focus on tasks that align with long-term objectives, facilitating a more measured approach to workload management that reduces unnecessary cognitive strain. This practice not only optimizes individual performance but also fosters a culture in which strategic thinking is valued over impulsive action.

Implementing structured prioritization techniques can help managers mitigate the risk of cognitive overload among their teams, ultimately improving both performance and job satisfaction. These techniques align with contemporary psychological insights into cognitive functioning, showing how the brain operates most effectively when given time for focused attention and recovery. Proper prioritization also strengthens attentional control, the cognitive process responsible for directing mental focus to relevant information while filtering out distractions. Attentional control is essential for maintaining a sense of balance amid competing priorities, enabling individuals to navigate high-pressure situations without succumbing to mental fatigue. In doing so, managers cultivate an environment where employees can perform optimally, adapt to shifting demands, and sustain productivity over the long term.

Incorporating prioritization strategies like the Eisenhower Matrix, task batching, and time-blocking into daily workflows not only reduces cognitive load but also enhances overall business processes. Managers who prioritize effectively are better equipped to allocate resources, streamline decision-making, and delegate tasks, ensuring that team efforts are concentrated on meaningful work. This strategic approach promotes a cycle of efficiency and focus, reinforcing a mindset of proactive management that supports both individual and organizational resilience.

Strategic Delegation

The psychological impact of the strategic delegation process is substantial: when tasks are thoughtfully assigned to those with the most fitting skill sets, cognitive load is significantly reduced, not only for the manager but also for the entire team. This realignment of tasks allows managers to maintain a clearer focus, enhance decision quality, and ultimately preserve mental bandwidth for strategic thinking and problem-solving.

One of the fundamental elements of effective delegation is the alignment of tasks with team members' strengths and expertise. Assigning responsibilities based on individual skill sets maximizes performance while reducing the mental strain involved in performing unfamiliar or demanding tasks. This approach recognizes the varying capacities and competencies within the team, enabling each person to operate within their cognitive "comfort zone," where they can engage more deeply and effectively. In modern-day project management, this process of skills alignment is essential not only for productivity but also for creating an environment of cognitive ease in which individuals can perform with minimal stress and maximum effectiveness.

Delegation also requires overcoming the "delegation dilemma," a common hesitation among managers who may worry about relinquishing control over specific tasks. This reluctance can stem from underlying cognitive biases, such as the illusion of control, where managers feel that their direct involvement is necessary for quality assurance. Addressing this dilemma involves understanding that trust-building is fundamental to effective delegation. By recognizing their own tendencies toward cognitive overload, managers can appreciate the importance of distributing responsibilities and foster an atmosphere of trust. When managers trust their teams to handle specific tasks autonomously, they free up their own cognitive resources and encourage a shared ownership mindset among team members. A critical aspect of strategic delegation involves creating structured processes that support seamless handoffs of responsibility.

Setting clear expectations, defining roles, and providing context for tasks allow team members to understand the scope and significance of their assignments. This transparency not only enhances their ability to execute tasks effectively but also reduces the mental strain that can arise from ambiguity or unclear directives. By clearly outlining each team member's role, managers can prevent confusion and cognitive friction, fostering a workflow that minimizes unnecessary stressors. Such procedural clarity reinforces team members' confidence, enabling them to approach tasks with a higher level of engagement and focus.

Furthermore, delegation should be accompanied by feedback mechanisms that encourage continuous improvement. Providing constructive feedback helps team members refine their skills, making them even better suited to handle specific responsibilities in the future. This process of skill enhancement and feedback ensures that delegation does not just lighten cognitive load in the short term but also strengthens team capabilities over time. When feedback loops are in place, team members feel supported and understood, reducing defensive reactions and allowing them to build resilience in their roles. To make delegation even more effective, managers should be aware of the psychological concept of cognitive congruence, which suggests that people perform optimally when the complexity of tasks matches their cognitive capacity. By ensuring that tasks are matched to individuals based on cognitive congruence, managers can help prevent cognitive overload and promote a sustainable workload distribution across the team. This alignment between task complexity and individual capability supports optimal productivity without compromising mental well-being.

In addition to workload distribution, strategic delegation also taps into the psychological concept of social proof, where individuals feel motivated to perform when they observe others successfully handling responsibilities. By assigning tasks and responsibilities publicly within the team, managers can leverage social proof to inspire team members to rise to the occasion. When delegation is visible and celebrated, team members are likely to experience increased confidence and motivation, knowing that they are trusted to take on important tasks. This collective sense of responsibility not only reinforces individual performance but also cultivates a culture of mutual support, where each team member feels accountable and engaged.

The broader impact of delegation extends beyond cognitive relief for the manager. By involving team members in the decision-making process, managers foster a culture of autonomy and empowerment that benefits the entire team. Team members who are given the freedom to make decisions within their areas of responsibility develop a stronger sense of ownership and commitment. This autonomy supports intrinsic motivation, which is essential for sustaining long-term engagement and resilience in dynamic work environments. When team members feel that their contributions are valued, they are more likely to approach tasks with a proactive mindset, which in turn alleviates cognitive strain for the manager by reducing the need for constant oversight.

To sustain the positive outcomes of delegation, managers should also implement regular check-ins that focus on alignment and provide an opportunity for open communication. These check-ins create a framework for ongoing dialogue, where both managers and team members can address any evolving needs, skill adjustments, or workload concerns. By consistently engaging with team members through structured check-ins, managers can anticipate challenges, identify gaps in skills or resources, and make necessary adjustments to keep cognitive load manageable. This proactive approach strengthens the delegation process by ensuring that each team member is both equipped and prepared to handle their responsibilities effectively.

Strategic delegation is not merely a means of reducing cognitive load; it is a process that requires psychological insight, trust-building, and procedural clarity. Managers can align team members' strengths with specific responsibilities and optimize workload distribution while fostering an environment of cognitive ease.

Reducing Cognitive Fragmentation

Reducing cognitive fragmentation is a critical yet often overlooked strategy for sustaining strategic focus in management roles. Project managers, in particular, are tasked with navigating myriad small, repetitive decisions that collectively contribute to cognitive overload. These micro-decisions, while minor individually, accumulate over the course of a day or week, creating what is often termed "cognitive fragmentation." The mental energy expended on such decisions is not easily replenished and, over time, can hinder a manager's ability to sustain focus, creativity, and strategic thinking. This subchapter focuses on understanding the impact of cognitive fragmentation and implementing strategies to reduce it, thus preserving a manager's mental bandwidth for high-priority tasks and complex decision-making.

One key to addressing cognitive fragmentation is recognizing the toll that micro-decisions take on cognitive resources. Micro-decisions are often reactionary responses—such as answering routine questions, approving minor requests, or deciding on small administrative details—which may seem insignificant but collectively drain cognitive energy. When faced with multiple micro-decisions, a manager's brain must constantly switch between contexts, which studies show increases cognitive fatigue and reduces working memory capacity. This phenomenon, known as the "task-switching cost," can lead to mental strain and even decision paralysis over time, impairing the ability to handle larger tasks that require sustained attention and problem-solving. To mitigate this, leaders need to implement strategies that structure and streamline these micro-decisions, preserving mental resources for high-level thinking.

A core strategy for managing micro-decisions is task grouping, a time-management technique designed to consolidate similar tasks into designated intervals. By grouping micro-decisions, managers can address them in batches rather than scattering them throughout the day, which reduces the cognitive demand of context-switching and allows for deeper concentration on larger priorities. Task grouping also facilitates the establishment of "focus blocks," periods of uninterrupted time dedicated solely to strategic projects or complex issues. When applied consistently, focus blocks prevent cognitive fragmentation by ensuring that high-level tasks are shielded from the constant disruptions that micro-decisions can introduce. Managers should consider allocating specific times of the day for addressing routine decisions, delegating them when possible, or even automating them to free up mental resources for core responsibilities.

Streamlined decision-making routines are another critical element for reducing cognitive fragmentation. Managers can develop predefined protocols for handling frequently recurring micro-decisions, allowing them to bypass the need for constant mental evaluation. For instance, implementing standardized processes for approvals or routine inquiries reduces the cognitive load associated with each decision, as they no longer require individualized analysis. This approach can also involve creating structured guidelines or criteria for the team, enabling them to autonomously make smaller decisions that align with the manager's strategic objectives. When team members understand the parameters within which they can operate independently, it minimizes the need for manager intervention, thus preserving mental bandwidth.

The role of organizational structure in cognitive management cannot be overstated. Managers benefit from fostering a supportive team environment that prioritizes collaborative problem-solving and minimizes unnecessary interruptions. When a team is encouraged to take ownership of its tasks and work independently within defined guidelines, it decreases the number of decisions that are escalated to the manager. Cultivating a culture of self-sufficiency and delegation not only reduces cognitive fragmentation for the manager but also empowers the team to engage actively in the decision-making process, enhancing overall productivity. Managers should work to create clear communication channels and structured feedback loops that allow team members to address routine issues autonomously, knowing they have support from leadership without needing constant supervision.

In addition to structural adjustments, managers can adopt mindfulness techniques to enhance cognitive resilience, which can be integral for maintaining mental clarity in the face of daily micro-decisions. Mindfulness training and focused attention practices help improve a leader's capacity to stay centered and resist the pull of cognitive fragmentation. Studies indicate that mindfulness improves cognitive control, enabling managers to be more intentional about where they allocate their mental resources and to recognize when they are approaching cognitive fatigue.

Practicing mindfulness also promotes emotional regulation, which assists managers in responding calmly to external demands without succumbing to the mental drain of reactionary decision-making. Incorporating brief moments of pause throughout the day, especially before transitioning between tasks, can help recalibrate mental focus, allowing managers to approach each decision with renewed clarity.

Lastly, managers should prioritize the development of time-blocking methods that align with their cognitive peak periods. Research has shown that cognitive performance fluctuates throughout the day, often following patterns related to individual circadian rhythms. Identifying periods when cognitive energy is highest and scheduling focus blocks during these times maximizes a manager's ability to engage with strategic tasks at full capacity. Conversely, allocating less demanding micro-decisions to periods of lower cognitive energy can help maintain mental stamina throughout the day. By aligning decision-making with natural energy cycles, managers reduce the likelihood of cognitive fragmentation and ensure that their most challenging work receives optimal attention. This sophisticated approach is not merely a matter of time management; it is cognitive resource allocation that requires thoughtful planning and disciplined execution.

Managing Cognitive Load in Multicultural Teams

In today's global business environment, leaders are increasingly tasked with guiding diverse teams, each bringing unique cultural perspectives that, while enriching, also increase the cognitive demands on managers. Effective leadership in such environments involves bridging communication styles and aligning objectives without compromising individual cultural integrity. The cognitive strain introduced by such diversity can be substantial, yet it is manageable through deliberate strategies aimed at understanding and integrating intercultural nuances to enhance cohesion and reduce misunderstandings.

One of the primary cognitive challenges for managers of multicultural teams is navigating diverse communication styles. Cultural heritage, racial background, and ethnicity can strongly influence how individuals communicate, interpret messages, and perceive feedback. For example, high-context cultures, such as those in parts of Asia, Africa, and Latin America, tend to rely heavily on implicit communication, where much of the meaning is conveyed through context, body language, and tone rather than explicit words. Low-context cultures, such as those prevalent in North America and parts of Europe, typically rely on direct, straightforward language where messages are explicit and detailed. This variation requires leaders to adapt their communication strategies, balancing between implicit and explicit messaging as appropriate.

For managers, this cultural bridging demands heightened cognitive flexibility, as they must process and interpret not only the message itself but also the underlying cultural context. Adopting active listening practices and mirroring team members' communication styles can alleviate some of the cognitive load associated with decoding culturally nuanced messages. By aligning communication methods more closely with cultural expectations, managers reduce the cognitive strain that comes with constant interpretation, fostering clearer, more efficient exchanges. Additionally, encouraging open discussions about communication preferences within the team creates a foundation of mutual understanding, allowing for smoother and more cohesive interactions.

Time perception is another culturally influenced factor that impacts cognitive load in multicultural teams. Different cultures may have varying views on time management, deadlines, and pacing. For instance, some cultures operate with a monochronic time orientation, where time is perceived linearly and schedules are strictly followed. Others follow a polychronic orientation, viewing time as more flexible, with less emphasis on rigid deadlines. This discrepancy can cause tension if expectations around time are not clearly communicated and mutually agreed upon. To manage the cognitive strain of balancing these perceptions, leaders benefit from establishing a clear but culturally sensitive framework for time management that respects both monochronic and polychronic tendencies. Setting flexible yet well-defined timelines helps bridge this gap, enabling team members to adapt their work approaches to a cohesive schedule without feeling culturally pressured. By making time-related expectations explicit and aligning them with the team's collective goals, managers reduce the need for constant recalibration and create a sense of predictability that mitigates cognitive strain. Leadership authority is also perceived differently across cultures, adding another layer to cognitive load. In hierarchical cultures, authority figures are often viewed with high regard, and decisions made by managers may not be questioned or challenged openly. In contrast, more egalitarian cultures encourage open dialogue and expect decisions to be collaborative. For managers leading multicultural teams, this creates a cognitive dilemma, as they must continually adjust their leadership style to meet diverse expectations around authority while maintaining team cohesion.

To ease this cognitive burden, leaders should clarify their decision-making approach upfront and create space for cultural discussions around authority. Articulating one's leadership style and inviting team members to share their own cultural views on authority fosters mutual respect. By doing so, managers alleviate the cognitive load associated with interpreting unspoken cultural cues and create an environment where authority is understood and accepted within culturally appropriate boundaries. This alignment helps reduce cognitive tension and establishes a clear operational structure that supports team performance.

Managing cognitive load also involves cultivating a supportive environment where cultural differences are acknowledged and valued. Recognizing the unique strengths that each cultural perspective brings to the team enhances inclusivity and reduces feelings of alienation among team members. By fostering psychological safety—where individuals feel secure to express themselves without fear of negative repercussions—managers allow for open exchanges of ideas and perspectives, which strengthens team cohesion. This psychological safety not only eases cognitive load for team members, as they do not feel compelled to constantly self-monitor, but also enables the leader to direct their mental resources toward strategic goals rather than interpersonal conflict resolution.

Moreover, effective management of cognitive load in multicultural teams requires the integration of frameworks that facilitate intercultural awareness and understanding. Providing cultural training sessions or workshops that educate team members on the diverse backgrounds within the group promotes empathy and minimizes misunderstandings. When teams are equipped with an understanding of cultural differences, they experience fewer instances of misinterpretation and confusion, further reducing the cognitive strain on the manager who would otherwise need to mediate these issues. Managers can also use digital tools designed to support asynchronous work, which respects both time zone differences and cultural preferences for work pacing, thereby reducing the pressure on team members to conform to a uniform standard.

The cumulative effect of managing cognitive load in multicultural teams is a more cohesive, resilient group capable of navigating complexity with agility and insight. Leaders who proactively address cognitive fragmentation stemming from cultural diversity set a standard of inclusivity and foster an environment where team members feel valued. Recognizing and addressing the impact of culture on communication, time management, and authority, managers are better positioned to reduce cognitive strain and lead their teams with clarity and purpose. These techniques support sustained focus, strategic thinking, and resilience, enabling leaders to make thoughtful, impactful decisions and drive their teams forward with clarity and purpose.

Try This: Actionable Steps for Managing Cognitive Load and Time Effectively

1. Combat Multitasking with Focused Work Strategies

- **Exercise: Single-Task Timer**: Choose one task and set a timer for 25 minutes (using the Pomodoro Technique). During this time, eliminate distractions and focus solely on the task. When the timer ends, take a 5-minute break before starting the next task. Gradually extend focus intervals as you build concentration.

- **Action: Batch Similar Tasks Together**: Group similar activities (e.g., emails, meetings, or brainstorming) into dedicated blocks of time. For instance, schedule all calls in the afternoon to keep the morning for deep work.

- **Create a "Distraction Notebook"**: Keep a notebook nearby to jot down intrusive thoughts or unrelated tasks. This allows you to acknowledge distractions without derailing your focus.

2. Reduce Cognitive Overload Through Prioritization

- **Exercise: The Eisenhower Matrix**: Create a four-quadrant matrix labeled: Urgent and Important, Important but Not Urgent, Urgent but Not Important, and Neither. Categorize your tasks accordingly and focus first on those in the "Urgent and Important" quadrant.

- **Action: Adopt a "Big Three" Approach**: At the start of each day, identify your top three priorities. Write them down and structure your workday to ensure they get done.

- **Defer or Eliminate Low-Impact Tasks**: Regularly review your to-do list to identify tasks that don't align with your goals. Ask, *"Does this truly need my attention, or can it wait or be removed altogether?"*

3. Master Strategic Delegation

- **Exercise: Delegation Map**
- List your tasks and identify those that:
  - Require your unique skills (you handle).
  - Can be done by someone else (delegate).
  - Don't need immediate attention (defer).
  - Clearly outline the tasks to delegate and assign them to team members with detailed instructions.

- **Action: Use the 70% Rule for Delegation**: If a team member can perform a task at least 70% as well as you can, delegate it. This empowers others while freeing you to focus on higher-priority responsibilities.

- **Establish Feedback Loops**: Create a system where team members can provide updates and ask questions without micromanagement. For example, schedule short, weekly check-ins for progress reviews.

4. Minimize Cognitive Fragmentation

- **Exercise: Schedule "Deep Work" Time**: Block out two uninterrupted hours daily for complex, high-value tasks. Label this time on your calendar to signal its importance and avoid interruptions.

- **Action: Designate Communication Windows**: Set specific times to check emails and messages rather than responding throughout the day. Inform your team of these windows to manage expectations.

- **Use Digital Tools Wisely**: Limit the number of apps or platforms you use. Consolidate tools for task management, communication, and project tracking into as few systems as possible.

5. Manage Cognitive Load in Multicultural Teams

- **Exercise: Cross-Cultural Feedback Practices**: Conduct a team workshop where members share preferred communication and work styles. This fosters mutual understanding and reduces miscommunication.

- **Action: Adjust Task Complexity for Diverse Teams**: Break large, complex tasks into smaller, clearly defined steps with context that accommodates varying cultural approaches to problem-solving.

- **Utilize Visual Tools for Clarity**: Use visuals like flowcharts, diagrams, or timelines to enhance understanding across language barriers and cognitive styles.

Reflect and Act

Effectively managing cognitive load and time isn't just a personal skill—it's a leadership imperative. By implementing these practices, you'll enhance your own productivity while fostering a more focused, balanced, and efficient team environment.

Case Study 1: Overcoming Multitasking Pitfalls to Boost Productivity

Scenario:

Jordan is a team leader responsible for coordinating multiple projects simultaneously. His day is often fragmented by constant task-switching between meetings, emails, and planning sessions, leaving him mentally drained and feeling unproductive. Jordan realizes that his multitasking habits are hindering his ability to focus on high-priority tasks and make effective decisions.

Questions:

1. What steps can Jordan take to reduce the negative impact of multitasking on his productivity and mental clarity?

2. How might Jordan restructure his day to prioritize deep work while managing his ongoing responsibilities?

3. What psychological strategies can Jordan implement to improve his focus and avoid decision fatigue?

Case Study 2: Prioritization Challenges in a Multicultural Team

Scenario:

Anika manages a multicultural team spread across different time zones, with varying cultural attitudes toward deadlines, hierarchy, and task prioritization. She often finds herself struggling to align the team's expectations and workflow, leading to delays and misunderstandings. Anika needs to find effective ways to prioritize tasks and foster alignment across her diverse team.

Questions:

1. How can Anika leverage prioritization techniques to create a shared understanding of team goals and deadlines?

2. What strategies can Anika use to accommodate cultural differences while maintaining efficiency and cohesion?

3. How might fostering open communication and mutual respect improve the team's time management and overall productivity?

Case Study 3: Delegating Strategically to Manage Cognitive Overload

Scenario:

Carlos, a department head, frequently takes on more tasks than he can handle because he believes no one else can complete them to his standards. As a result, Carlos is experiencing cognitive overload, which affects his ability to think strategically and support his team effectively. He knows he needs to delegate more but struggles to trust his team members with critical tasks.

Questions:

1. How can Carlos identify tasks that can be delegated without compromising quality or control?

2. What psychological factors might be contributing to Carlos's reluctance to delegate, and how can he address them?

3. How can Carlos build trust within his team to ensure successful delegation and reduce his cognitive load?

Reflective Component

I encourage you to:

- Reflect on your own challenges with multitasking, prioritization, or delegation.
- Write down three specific actions you can take to improve your time management and reduce cognitive overload.
- Consider how integrating these strategies could enhance your productivity and leadership effectiveness.

Chapter 8
The Physical Price of Stress

Stress is an unavoidable component of life, especially in professional environments where leaders and managers navigate high expectations, tight deadlines, and continuous decision-making. While stress can be a motivating force, prolonged and unaddressed stress accumulates and takes a significant toll on the body, affecting not only physical health but also cognitive and emotional well-being. In understanding the physical price of stress, it becomes clear that managing stress is not just an individual responsibility; managers play a crucial role in recognizing the signs of burnout and promoting stress relief practices within their teams. Encouraging self-care, creating a supportive work environment, and implementing practices like scheduled vacations and reduced workloads are not just optional enhancements but necessities for sustainable health, productivity, and organizational success.

How Stress Physically Impacts the Body

The body's response to stress is rooted in the "fight-or-flight" reaction, a survival mechanism that releases hormones such as cortisol and adrenaline to help an individual respond to immediate threats. While beneficial in short bursts, this system is not designed for prolonged activation. Continuous, high-stress environments lead to sustained elevations in cortisol levels, which have a destructive impact on various systems within the body, breaking down physical resilience and leaving individuals vulnerable to a multitude of health complications. Over time, this state of chronic activation increases the risk of cardiovascular issues such as high blood pressure and heart disease. Elevated cortisol contributes to the constriction of blood vessels, a response initially intended to prepare the body for immediate action. However, in a non-emergency setting, this process creates unnecessary strain on the heart and circulatory system, eventually manifesting in hypertension or, in more severe cases, conditions such as heart attacks and strokes. As managers and leaders often endure prolonged periods of stress, their risk of such conditions heightens, especially if stress management is neglected.

Immunosuppression: The Weakened Defense System

Another primary physical impact of stress is its suppression of the immune system. The human body prioritizes energy for immediate survival during stressful events, redirecting resources away from functions like immunity that are deemed less critical in urgent situations. In a workplace environment, however, sustained stress leads to compromised immunity over time, making individuals more susceptible to common illnesses, including colds, influenza, and viral infections. A weakened immune response not only affects individual health but also the organization's productivity, as increased sick days and lower energy levels slow progress toward team and company goals.

From a managerial perspective, encouraging team members to address and manage stress isn't just about showing empathy; it is a fundamental strategy for sustaining workforce productivity.

Leaders who proactively support employee health can help mitigate productivity losses that arise from immune-compromised employees who need significant time off to recover from illness. Promoting stress reduction techniques, regular health check-ups, and work-life balance can help protect employees from frequent illnesses and the cyclical strain these places on the team.

Muscle Tension, Headaches, and the Physical Strain of Mental Burden

Mental strain often expresses itself physically, particularly in the form of muscle tension, headaches, and migraines. Stress-induced muscle tension is commonly experienced in the shoulders, neck, and back, a result of the body's preparation for action that never actually materializes. Prolonged tension of this nature contributes to chronic pain and increases susceptibility to conditions like tension headaches and migraines, further compounding an individual's experience of stress. In the business world, leaders should recognize the signs of chronic physical stress in their employees and encourage a culture that acknowledges these physical symptoms rather than disregarding them. Managers should also consider the value of ergonomic resources, stress-relief breaks, and access to physical wellness resources, which can mitigate the onset of such physical manifestations. When the work environment itself contributes to physical discomfort, employees' cognitive clarity and overall productivity suffer. Alleviating physical stress, therefore, is directly linked to enhancing mental performance and supporting team morale.

The Connection Between Chronic Stress and Sleep Disorders

One of the most widespread consequences of prolonged stress is sleep disruption. Mental strain stimulates the mind and body, making it difficult to relax and maintain restful sleep cycles. Over time, chronic stress contributes to insomnia, fragmented sleep, and a general decline in sleep quality. Lack of sleep further compounds stress by impairing cognitive clarity, focus, and emotional resilience, leading to a feedback loop where stress and sleep deprivation fuel each other. Leaders who promote work cultures that emphasize proper sleep hygiene, encourage reasonable work hours, and discourage after-hours communication can help employees maintain healthier sleep patterns. To be effective in the long term, companies may also implement policies that support flexibility in work schedules, acknowledging that stress and sleep needs vary from person to person. These policies demonstrate that the organization values employee well-being, creating a supportive culture where individuals can reach their full potential.

Metabolic Effects of Stress: Implications for Long-Term Health

Stress influences the body's metabolism in ways that can lead to long-term health complications. Under stress, the body often releases additional glucose to provide immediate energy, which can lead to erratic blood sugar levels. When sustained, this response increases the risk of insulin resistance, a precursor to conditions such as type 2 diabetes. Chronic stress also influences appetite regulation, potentially causing individuals to overeat as a form of stress relief. These factors contribute to unhealthy weight fluctuations, which in turn can increase the risk of cardiovascular disease and metabolic disorders.

The effects of stress on metabolism further highlight the importance of a proactive approach to stress management within leadership roles. Managers should be aware of how metabolic stressors manifest in behaviors such as overeating, frequent snacking, or the misuse of stimulants like caffeine. Organizations that promote healthy eating, physical activity, and stress management workshops can help employees manage these stress-induced tendencies, ultimately supporting a healthier, more productive workforce.

Cognitive Clarity, Decision-Making, and Emotional Resilience Under Stress

Beyond physical health, chronic stress impairs cognitive clarity, decision-making, and emotional resilience. Leaders frequently make critical decisions that require clear thinking, sound judgment, and emotional balance. However, chronic stress impacts these abilities by clouding mental clarity, decreasing memory retention, and impairing problem-solving skills. Over time, stress can erode emotional resilience, making leaders and employees more prone to impulsive reactions, irritability, and burnout. The result is a cycle where stress impedes effective decision-making, leading to suboptimal choices and additional stressors, perpetuating a downward spiral of mental and physical health deterioration.

For leaders, maintaining cognitive clarity under stress is vital. By developing mental boundaries, practicing mindfulness, and regularly assessing stress levels, leaders can prevent the decline in cognitive function that prolonged stress often causes. Furthermore, integrating practices that support mental clarity—

such as reflective thinking and planning time—into organizational routines can help leaders sustain high levels of performance.

Recommended Practices for Safeguarding Health and Promoting Stress Relief

To mitigate the impact of stress on the physical and mental health of employees, modern companies have adopted policies and programs that allow individuals to balance work demands with self-care. Managers should be familiar with these practices, both to safeguard their own well-being and to set an example for their teams.

1. **Encouraging Vacation and Time Off**: Taking time away from work is essential for recovery and rejuvenation. Vacations allow individuals to reset their mental and physical states, improving productivity and motivation upon return. Managers should encourage employees to utilize their vacation days and refrain from creating an environment where taking time off is implicitly discouraged. Allowing individuals to take time off without fear of negative repercussions supports a healthy and resilient workforce.

2. **Providing Access to Counseling and Mental Health Services**: Mental health resources, such as counseling and Employee Assistance Programs (EAPs), offer individuals a safe space to manage and reduce stress. Managers who normalize the use of these resources encourage employees to address their mental health proactively. In organizations that value mental health, leaders set the tone by being open about the importance of such services, reducing any stigma associated with seeking help.

3. **Implementing Flexible Work Arrangements**: Flexible work hours and remote work options allow individuals to tailor their schedules to suit personal needs, reducing stress that arises from rigid or extended work hours. Flexibility in scheduling helps individuals manage personal commitments, avoid burnout, and maintain a balance between work and life responsibilities, supporting better physical and mental health.

4. **Reducing Workloads During High-Stress Periods**: In times of elevated stress, managers should consider redistributing workloads to prevent individual burnout. Workload management may involve setting clearer priorities, delegating tasks, or rescheduling non-essential projects. By proactively reducing workloads, leaders can help employees maintain productivity without risking their health.

5. **Incorporating Regular Breaks and Downtime**: Breaks are essential for sustaining cognitive function and physical health throughout the workday. Research supports the importance of regular intervals of rest, showing that even short breaks can significantly improve mental clarity, focus, and emotional balance. By building breaks into daily schedules and discouraging work during downtime, managers can create a healthier work environment.

6. **Promoting a Culture of Mindfulness and Well-Being**: Mindfulness practices, such as meditation and focused breathing, offer employees effective ways to reduce stress and build emotional resilience. Organizations that implement mindfulness programs and provide resources for practicing mindfulness empower employees to take ownership of their well-being. Managers who lead by

example and incorporate mindfulness into their routines can enhance their ability to handle stress and set a positive precedent for the team.

Prioritizing Well-Being as a Pillar of Effective Leadership

The toll of chronic stress on the body is profound, affecting nearly every physical and mental system. High-stress work environments amplify this effect, as continuous pressure erodes physical health, reduces immune response, and impairs cognitive clarity. For leaders, recognizing and addressing stress is not only an individual responsibility but a key aspect of effective management. By encouraging self-care practices and supporting an environment where physical and mental health are prioritized, leaders create a sustainable foundation for personal success and team productivity.

Ultimately, managing stress in a leadership role requires a proactive approach that includes personal stress reduction techniques and organizational support. Leaders who prioritize well-being demonstrate that health is an essential aspect of professional success, fostering a culture where employees feel supported in managing stress. This emphasis on health and well-being cultivates resilience and supports long-term organizational productivity, ensuring that both leaders and employees are equipped to handle the challenges of a demanding workplace.

Try This: Actionable Steps for Managing Stress and Prioritizing Well-Being

1. Recognize Stress and Its Physical Symptoms

- **Exercise: Daily Stress Log**: At the end of each day, jot down moments that triggered stress. Note physical symptoms (e.g., headaches, fatigue) and the circumstances. Over time, identify patterns and high-stress situations to address proactively.

- **Action: Check Your Body's Signals**: Set a timer every two hours during your workday. When it goes off, pause and scan your body. Are your shoulders tense? Is your breathing shallow? Use this awareness to adjust posture, stretch, or take deep breaths.

2. Combat Immunosuppression Through Lifestyle Adjustments

- **Exercise: Hydration and Nutrition Tracker**: Use a simple app or notebook to monitor water intake and meals. Ensure your diet includes immune-supporting foods rich in vitamins C and E, zinc, and antioxidants.

- **Action: Build Immunity Through Rest**: Prioritize sleep hygiene. Set a consistent bedtime, minimize screen time an hour before sleep, and create a relaxing routine such as reading or meditation. Use white noise or blackout curtains if needed.

3. Relieve Muscle Tension and Physical Strain

- **Exercise: The 5-Minute Stretch Break**: Schedule short breaks every hour. Incorporate stretches targeting the neck, shoulders, and back—common areas of stress tension. Simple desk stretches or yoga poses can provide relief.

- **Action: Ergonomic Workspace Audit**: Assess your desk setup. Adjust your chair, desk height, and monitor to promote proper posture and reduce physical strain. Consider standing desks or supportive cushions as needed.

4. Address Sleep and Cognitive Clarity

- **Exercise: Pre-Sleep Gratitude Journal**: Before bed, write down three things you're grateful for. This practice calms the mind, reduces stress, and promotes better sleep.

- **Action: Establish a "Shutdown Routine"** : Create an end-of-day ritual to separate work from personal life. This might include shutting off devices, setting priorities for the next day, or engaging in a relaxing activity like reading or listening to music.

5. Build Emotional Resilience Under Stress

- **Exercise: "Reframe the Challenge" Journal**: When faced with a stressful situation, write down the issue, your initial emotional response, and an alternative perspective. For example, instead of seeing a tough deadline as overwhelming, view it as an opportunity to showcase efficiency.

- **Action: Practice Regular Mindfulness**: Dedicate 5–10 minutes daily to mindfulness exercises like guided meditation or focused breathing. Apps like Calm or Headspace can help cultivate this habit.

6. Implement Workplace Stress-Relief Practices

- **Exercise: Promote Break Culture**: As a leader or team member, encourage regular, brief breaks during high-stress periods. Share stress-relief techniques with your team, such as guided stretches or mindfulness exercises.

- **Action: Advocate for Flexibility**: Work with management to implement flexible work arrangements, such as adjustable hours or remote work opportunities, to reduce stress for yourself and your team.

7. Lead by Example in Prioritizing Well-Being

- **Exercise: Personal Stress-Relief Commitment**: Publicly share your commitment to stress management with your team. For instance, let them know you'll step away for a brief walk or mindfulness break when stressed. This normalizes self-care in the workplace.

- **Action: Foster a Culture of Support**: Encourage an open-door policy for mental health concerns. Create a space where team members feel comfortable discussing stressors and seeking support without judgment.

Reflect and Act

Stress is an unavoidable aspect of modern work, but it doesn't have to be debilitating. By actively managing stress and prioritizing well-being, you can improve physical health, foster mental clarity, and inspire your team to do the same.

Self-Assessment: Navigating Change, Cognitive Load, and Stress Management

This self-assessment helps you reflect on your ability to handle resistance, manage time effectively, and prioritize health amidst workplace challenges. Answer the following questions honestly to identify strengths and areas for growth. Use the interpretations and strategies provided to enhance your effectiveness.

Instructions

Rate yourself on a scale of 1 to 5 for each statement:

1 = Strongly Disagree

2 = Disagree

3 = Neutral

4 = Agree

5 = Strongly Agree

Handling Resistance and Change

1. I empathize with team members' concerns during change and adjust my approach accordingly.

2. I recognize and address defensive behaviors in team members to minimize resistance.

3. I anticipate power dynamics that may arise during change and navigate them constructively.

4. I view resistance as an opportunity for growth and adapt processes based on constructive feedback.

5. I effectively reinforce new norms and behaviors to sustain long-term change.

Cognitive Load and Time Management

1. I recognize when I'm multitasking and adjust to focus on one task at a time to improve productivity.

2. I use prioritization tools (e.g., Eisenhower Matrix or task batching) to manage my workload effectively.

3. I delegate tasks appropriately to reduce my cognitive load and empower my team.

4. I minimize distractions and fragmentation by setting clear boundaries for focused work time.

5. I adapt my communication style to align with the needs of multicultural or diverse teams.

The Physical Price of Stress

1. I recognize the physical signs of stress in myself and take proactive measures to address them.

2. I incorporate regular breaks and downtime into my schedule to support mental clarity and physical well-being.

3. I maintain healthy habits, such as exercise, proper nutrition, and sufficient sleep, to mitigate the effects of stress.

4. I actively promote a culture of mindfulness and well-being within my team or organization.

5. I encourage team members to take time off, seek counseling, or adjust workloads when necessary to prevent burnout.

Scoring and Interpretation

1. **Total your scores for each section:**
   - *Handling Resistance and Change*: Questions 1-5
   - *Cognitive Load and Time Management*: Questions 6-10
   - *The Physical Price of Stress*: Questions 11-15

2. **Interpret your results using the ranges below:**

Handling Resistance and Change

- **21-25:** Excellent! You have a strong ability to navigate resistance and guide your team through change. Continue refining your approach by exploring advanced change management techniques.

- **16-20:** Good, but there's room for growth. Focus on deepening your empathy and reinforcing long-term behavioral changes.

- **15 or below:** Needs improvement. Begin by building trust and addressing resistance constructively.

Cognitive Load and Time Management

- **21-25:** Outstanding time management and cognitive load management skills. Consider mentoring others or implementing team-wide productivity practices.

- **16-20:** Solid foundation. Work on improving focus and delegation to enhance efficiency.

- **15 or below:** Requires development. Start with prioritization tools and focused work techniques to reduce cognitive strain.

The Physical Price of Stress

- **21-25:** Exceptional ability to manage stress and promote well-being. Maintain your habits and encourage team-wide adoption of these practices.

- **16-20:** Good progress. Strengthen your efforts by prioritizing physical health and encouraging stress reduction strategies in your team.

- **15 or below:** Needs attention. Begin by recognizing stress triggers and integrating small, consistent self-care habits.

Strategies for Improvement

Handling Resistance and Change

- **Empathy-Driven Management**: Conduct regular one-on-one check-ins with team members to address concerns and build trust.

- **Reframe Resistance**: When encountering resistance, ask, *"What can this feedback teach us about improving our process?"*

- **Sustain New Norms**: Use positive reinforcement, such as celebrating small wins, to solidify new behaviors.

Cognitive Load and Time Management

- **Focus Techniques**: Implement time-blocking to allocate uninterrupted periods for deep work.

- **Effective Delegation**: Match tasks to team members' strengths and clearly communicate expectations.

- **Cultural Communication**: Use visuals and shared tools to bridge cultural differences in communication styles.

The Physical Price of Stress

- **Health Prioritization**: Schedule at least 30 minutes of physical activity daily and practice mindfulness exercises.

- **Stress Awareness**: Use a stress journal to identify triggers and track physical symptoms over time.

- **Team Wellness Culture**: Advocate for flexible work policies and access to mental health resources within your organization.

Reflect and Act

Your ability to navigate change, manage mental and physical well-being, and prioritize effectively will directly impact your success as a leader. Use this self-assessment periodically to measure your growth and refine your approach.

Case Study 1: Recognizing the Impact of Stress on Decision-Making and Team Dynamics

Scenario:

Samantha, a senior manager, is under significant pressure to deliver results on a critical project. Her mounting stress has begun to affect her decision-making clarity, leading to rushed choices and occasional errors. Samantha's team members are noticing her heightened irritability and feel hesitant to approach her with concerns, further straining the work environment.

Questions:

1. How might chronic stress be impacting Samantha's cognitive clarity and decision-making abilities?

2. What are the potential ripple effects of Samantha's stress on her team's morale and performance?

3. What strategies can Samantha implement to manage her stress and improve her leadership effectiveness?

Case Study 2: Addressing Physical Symptoms of Stress in Leadership

Scenario:

James, a department head, has been experiencing frequent headaches, muscle tension, and fatigue. He attributes these symptoms to long hours and heavy workloads but continues to push himself without taking breaks or delegating tasks. Despite his best efforts, James's productivity is declining, and his health issues are worsening, affecting his ability to lead effectively.

Questions:

1. How might James's physical symptoms of stress be connected to his mental strain and workload?

2. What practices could James adopt to safeguard his health and maintain sustainable productivity?

3. How could prioritizing his well-being positively influence James's leadership and team performance?

Case Study 3: Encouraging a Culture of Well-Being in the Workplace

Scenario:

Maria, a project director, notices that her team frequently skips lunch breaks and works overtime to meet deadlines. While productivity appears high, she observes increasing signs of burnout, such as absenteeism, irritability, and reduced engagement. Maria decides to promote a workplace culture that prioritizes mindfulness and well-being to support her team's long-term success.

Questions:

1. What specific steps can Maria take to create a culture that prioritizes mental and physical well-being?

2. How can Maria encourage her team to adopt healthy work habits without compromising productivity?

3. What role does modeling self-care play in Maria's ability to lead by example and inspire her team?

Reflective Component

I encourage you to:

- Reflect on your own experiences with stress, whether as a leader or team member, and how it has impacted your decision-making, health, and workplace dynamics.

- Identify three specific actions you can take to manage stress and foster a healthier work environment.

- Consider how prioritizing well-being could enhance your leadership and your team's long-term success.

Conclusion

As we reach the end of this book, it is vital to reflect on the journey we've taken through the intricate landscape of leadership and project management, focusing on the psychological aspects that significantly influence how managers navigate their roles. Throughout this exploration, we have come to understand the profound impact that mindset, emotional intelligence, and management styles have on both leaders and their teams. It's clear that a leader's mindset shapes not only their approach to challenges but also their ability to inspire, adapt, and guide their teams through ever-evolving circumstances. By cultivating a growth mindset, leaders can foster a culture of continuous improvement, resilience, and an openness to learning, which is essential for both personal and professional development. Additionally, emotional intelligence has emerged as a cornerstone of effective leadership. The ability to recognize, understand, and regulate one's own emotions, as well as the emotions of others, is crucial in building strong, supportive relationships within a team.

Emotionally intelligent leaders can create an environment where team members feel heard, valued, and empowered to contribute their best work. This contributes to a collaborative and cohesive team dynamic, where each individual's strengths are acknowledged and leveraged for collective success. The exploration of various management styles and their psychological impacts has provided valuable insights into how leaders can tailor their approaches to suit the unique needs of their teams. Recognizing the psychological effects of different leadership styles allows managers to adapt their methods to ensure they create the most conducive environment for team engagement, productivity, and growth. Equally important is understanding team dynamics. Teams are composed of individuals with unique personalities, communication styles, and motivations, and a leader's ability to navigate these dynamics determines their success in guiding the team toward its goals. Recognizing the interpersonal nuances that influence collaboration and conflict resolution can help leaders build a harmonious team that is capable of achieving outstanding results. When faced with resistance, whether it stems from fear of change or entrenched beliefs, the ability to manage and lead through these moments becomes critical. The psychological understanding of resistance allows leaders to approach change with empathy, communicate the vision effectively, and reduce apprehension, helping teams transition smoothly and remain focused on long-term objectives. Cognitive load management and time management are also integral to a leader's ability to maintain both personal and team effectiveness. In a world where constant demands and decision-making can easily lead to burnout, understanding the psychological limits of cognitive load and learning how to delegate, prioritize, and structure time effectively allows leaders to maintain clarity, focus, and energy. Finally, we discussed the often-overlooked consequences of stress, particularly the physical toll it takes on the body. Prolonged stress not only diminishes mental capacity and decision-making abilities but can also lead to severe health issues such as high blood pressure, heart disease, and weakened immune function. As a leader, understanding the mind-body connection is essential. Prioritizing self-care and implementing strategies to reduce stress not only enhances personal well-being but also ensures leaders can perform at their best, guiding their teams with clarity and purpose. The journey through these chapters has illuminated the essential skills and knowledge required for leadership in today's fast-paced, high-pressure world. The key takeaway is that leadership is not simply about managing tasks and people; it is about understanding oneself, the team, and the psychological factors that influence behavior and decision-making. Leaders who invest in developing emotional intelligence, maintaining a healthy mindset, and recognizing the importance of stress management will not only achieve success but will also create environments that empower their teams to thrive. The practices discussed in this book provide a strong foundation, but the journey of self-improvement and leadership is ongoing. For those seeking further clarification on specific terms or concepts, the glossary at the end of this book offers a comprehensive resource, providing additional insights to enhance your understanding. As you move forward, remember that leadership is a dynamic, evolving process that requires continual learning, self-reflection, and adaptability. By embracing these principles, you can not only improve your own leadership skills but also inspire and elevate those around you, creating a culture of success that extends beyond the workplace and into every aspect of life.

Appendix

Appendix 1-A: Answers and Insights for Chapter 1 Case Studies

Case Study 1: Creating a Behavioral Blueprint for Workplace Dynamics

1. How can Emily use personality assessments or behavioral theories to analyze the dynamics between her team members?

Emily can utilize tools such as the Big Five Personality Traits or the DISC Personality Assessment to better understand individual preferences and work styles. These assessments can provide insights into how each team member approaches tasks, communicates, and handles stress. Behavioral theories like Maslow's Hierarchy of Needs can also help Emily identify motivational drivers for each person, which will inform her strategies to align their goals with team objectives.

2. What strategies can she implement to align individual work styles with the team's overall objectives?

Emily should assign tasks that leverage each member's strengths while ensuring their work styles complement one another. For example, the structured team member can focus on detailed planning, while the improvisational team member handles brainstorming or adapting to unexpected changes. Emily should also facilitate open communication and establish team norms to ensure collaboration runs smoothly.

3. How might identifying patterns in team behavior help Emily predict and prevent future conflicts?

By observing patterns such as recurring miscommunications or delays in task handoffs, Emily can identify the root causes of conflict. For example, if disagreements arise during brainstorming sessions, Emily can introduce structured frameworks like Six Thinking Hats to guide discussions and reduce friction. Predicting these challenges allows her to proactively address issues before they escalate.

Case Study 2: Leveraging Psychological Forecasting for Strategic Decision-Making

1. What tools or methods can Alex use to forecast potential challenges and their impact on the project?

Alex can use tools such as scenario planning, SWOT analysis, or risk assessment matrices to anticipate challenges and prepare contingency plans. By consulting past project data and gathering feedback from his team, Alex can identify potential bottlenecks and resource gaps. Techniques like Monte Carlo simulations can also model risk probabilities for better forecasting.

2. How might cognitive biases, such as overconfidence or anchoring, affect his ability to predict risks accurately?

Overconfidence bias may cause Alex to underestimate potential risks or overestimate his team's ability to handle challenges, leading to insufficient planning. Anchoring bias could result in Alex fixating on initial estimates or assumptions, ignoring evolving project conditions. To counter these biases, Alex should seek diverse perspectives, encourage team feedback, and review decisions objectively.

3. What steps can Alex take to ensure his forecasting insights are actionable and communicated effectively to his team?

Alex should prioritize clear communication of risks and proposed solutions. Using visual tools like Gantt charts or risk heat maps can make forecasts more accessible. He should hold regular meetings to review progress, reassess risks, and adjust strategies as needed. Encouraging team input on forecasts ensures buy-in and collaborative problem-solving.

Case Study 3: Balancing Long-Term Vision with Immediate Team Needs

1. How can Maya use anticipatory thinking to address current challenges while aligning them with the department's long-term goals?

Maya can start by conducting a gap analysis to identify areas where current performance deviates from long-term goals. She should then prioritize immediate interventions, such as addressing workload imbalances or morale issues, that have the most significant impact on team capacity. Regularly revisiting the strategic plan ensures short-term actions remain aligned with overarching objectives.

2. What psychological factors, such as stress or burnout, might be influencing her team's performance, and how can she mitigate them?

Stress and burnout could stem from excessive workloads, lack of clarity, or feeling undervalued. Maya should implement strategies like workload redistribution, promoting psychological safety, and offering resources such as counseling or stress management workshops. Addressing these factors creates a more supportive environment, enabling the team to perform at their best.

3. How can Maya foster a growth mindset within her team to ensure they remain adaptable and engaged during the planning process?

Maya can encourage her team to view challenges as learning opportunities rather than setbacks. Celebrating small successes, offering continuous learning opportunities, and modeling adaptability herself can reinforce a growth mindset culture. Providing regular feedback focused on effort and improvement also helps the team stay motivated and resilient.

Appendix 2-A: Answers and Insights for Chapter 2 Case Studies

Case Study 1: Adapting to Change with Cognitive Flexibility

1. How can Laura use cognitive flexibility to reframe the situation and guide her team through this change effectively?

Laura can use cognitive flexibility by viewing the change as an opportunity for innovation rather than an obstacle. She should focus on the benefits of the new features and communicate these advantages to her team. Reframing the situation positively can help the team embrace the change and approach it with creativity and adaptability.

2. What steps can Laura take to ensure her team feels supported and motivated during this transition?

Laura should hold a team meeting to openly discuss the changes and provide a clear plan of action. Offering support through regular check-ins and encouraging team members to voice concerns fosters psychological safety. She can also delegate tasks aligned with individual strengths to maintain motivation and confidence.

3. How might Laura balance short-term task adjustments with the long-term vision of delivering a successful product?

Laura should create a revised project timeline that incorporates the new requirements while keeping the end goal in focus. She can break the project into smaller milestones, allowing the team to celebrate progress and stay aligned with the broader vision.

Case Study 2: Developing Emotional Intelligence to Resolve Team Tensions

1. What role does self-awareness play in how David approaches the conflict, and how can it help him set the right tone for resolution?

David's self-awareness allows him to recognize his own emotional triggers and biases, ensuring he approaches the conflict calmly and without judgment. By maintaining composure, he sets a constructive tone for resolution and models appropriate behavior for his team.

2. How can David apply empathy to understand the perspectives of the conflicting team members and foster mutual understanding?

David can schedule one-on-one conversations with each team member involved in the conflict. By actively listening and validating their feelings, he demonstrates empathy. Once he understands their perspectives, he can facilitate a dialogue where they identify common ground and work toward a resolution.

3. What specific social skills can David use to mediate the conflict and re-establish collaboration within his team?

David can use active listening and effective questioning to guide the discussion. Phrases like, *"Can you help me understand your perspective further?"* encourage openness. Additionally, he can establish ground rules for respectful communication during team meetings to rebuild trust and collaboration.

Case Study 3: Overcoming Self-Sabotaging Behaviors in Leadership

1. How can Sophia identify the underlying causes of her perfectionism and address them constructively?

Sophia should engage in self-reflection to explore the root causes of her perfectionism, such as fear of failure or lack of confidence. Journaling or working with a coach can help her identify patterns and shift her mindset toward valuing progress over perfection.

2. What strategies could Sophia use to delegate tasks more effectively while overcoming the urge to micromanage?

Sophia can adopt the 70% rule: if a team member can complete a task at least 70% as well as she would, she should delegate it. Providing clear instructions and establishing periodic check-ins allows her to maintain oversight without micromanaging, empowering her team to take ownership.

3. How might adopting a growth mindset help Sophia shift her focus from perfection to continuous improvement and team development?

By embracing a growth mindset, Sophia can focus on learning from mistakes and celebrating incremental progress. She can reframe challenges as opportunities for growth, both for herself and her team. Encouraging feedback and fostering a supportive environment further reinforce this mindset.

Appendix 3-A: Answers and Insights for Chapter 3 Case Studies

Case Study 1: Cognitive Restructuring in High-Stakes Leadership

Rebecca can begin by writing down her negative thoughts, such as *"I will fail this presentation"* or *"I am not good enough."* This externalization helps her recognize and separate these thoughts from reality. Once identified, she can examine whether these thoughts are based on facts or assumptions.

2. How can examining the evidence help Rebecca gain a more realistic perspective on her concerns?

By reflecting on past successes or feedback from colleagues, Rebecca can gather evidence that contradicts her negative beliefs. For instance, if she has successfully led similar presentations before, this evidence undermines her fear of failure. Identifying gaps between her fears and the reality helps shift her perspective.

3. What role does testing new, positive thoughts play in helping Rebecca build her confidence for the presentation?

Testing positive thoughts, such as *"I have prepared thoroughly and am capable of delivering this presentation,* "reinforces Rebecca's confidence. Practicing these thoughts through visualization or rehearsals strengthens her belief in her abilities, reducing anxiety and improving her performance.

Case Study 2: Emotional Regulation During a Workplace Crisis

1. What emotional regulation strategies can Jason use to maintain composure and clarity during this crisis?

Jason can use techniques like deep breathing or progressive muscle relaxation to calm his immediate physiological response to stress. He should also employ cognitive reappraisal, reframing the crisis as a challenge to be solved rather than an insurmountable failure. This mindset helps him approach the situation with a clear and solution-oriented attitude.

2. How can Jason's ability to regulate his emotions impact his team's response to the situation?

Jason's emotional regulation sets the tone for his team. By staying calm and composed, he models resilience, which reduces panic and fosters a sense of stability. His ability to manage his emotions creates a ripple effect, encouraging his team to focus on problem-solving rather than fear.

3. What steps can Jason take to help his team process their emotions and refocus on constructive solutions?

Jason can hold a team meeting to acknowledge the emotional impact of the crisis while providing a roadmap for addressing the issue. Encouraging open dialogue allows team members to express their concerns, while framing actionable steps helps them regain confidence and focus.

Case Study 3: Leveraging Emotional Contagion to Motivate a Team

1. How does emotional contagion play a role in Emma's ability to motivate her team during challenging times?

Emotional contagion refers to the phenomenon where one person's emotions influence others. Emma's enthusiasm, positivity, and energy can directly impact her team's mood and motivation. Conversely, if she displays negativity or stress, it could exacerbate the team's challenges.

2. What specific actions can Emma take to ensure her positive emotions inspire and energize her team?

Emma can start meetings with motivational messages or share success stories to boost morale. Regularly expressing gratitude and recognizing team achievements fosters positivity. Maintaining an optimistic yet realistic outlook on the project helps create a supportive and energized environment.

3. How can Emma balance emotional transparency with maintaining a professional and motivating demeanor?

Emma can acknowledge the team's challenges and her own frustrations, but she should quickly pivot to solutions and positive reinforcement. For example, instead of dwelling on tight deadlines, she could say, *"I understand this is challenging, but I know we can pull through because of our collective strengths."* This approach demonstrates authenticity while keeping the team focused.

Appendix 4-A: Answers and Insights for Chapter 4 Case Studies

Case Study 1: Balancing Transactional and Transformational Approaches

1. How can Ethan integrate transformational leadership principles while maintaining the structured benefits of transactional management?

Ethan can maintain transactional practices, like clear rewards and penalties, for short-term goals while incorporating transformational leadership techniques to inspire his team. This includes articulating a compelling vision for the team, encouraging innovation, and recognizing contributions beyond metrics. A balanced approach ensures the team feels both supported and motivated to achieve long-term growth.

2. What steps can Ethan take to improve team morale and foster a sense of purpose beyond short-term goals?

Ethan should prioritize open communication, asking team members about their career aspirations and aligning their work with personal growth opportunities. Hosting brainstorming sessions for new initiatives or encouraging feedback on team processes can give employees a greater sense of ownership and purpose. Recognizing effort, not just outcomes reinforces intrinsic motivation.

3. How might Ethan evaluate whether his leadership style is having a positive impact on the team's performance and engagement?

Ethan can use 360-degree feedback to gather insights from his team about their satisfaction and engagement. Regular check-ins and anonymous surveys can help him monitor morale and identify areas for improvement. Measuring turnover rates, employee engagement scores, and team productivity over time will also indicate whether his changes are effective.

Case Study 2: Addressing the Risks of Micromanagement

1. What psychological factors might be driving Olivia's micromanagement behavior, and how can she address them constructively?

Olivia's micromanagement may stem from a lack of trust in her team, fear of failure, or perfectionism. Recognizing these root causes is the first step. She can address them by acknowledging her team's competence, delegating small tasks initially to build confidence, and reminding herself that mistakes are part of growth.

2. How can Olivia rebuild trust and autonomy within her team while maintaining accountability?

Olivia can start by openly acknowledging her tendency to micromanage and expressing a commitment to change. She should assign team members tasks that align with their strengths and provide clear goals while allowing flexibility in execution. Establishing regular check-ins focused on progress rather than control fosters both accountability and autonomy.

3. What steps should Olivia take to transition to a more empowering leadership style, such as democratic or servant leadership?

Olivia can involve her team in decision-making by seeking their input on strategies and solutions. Practicing servant leadership by prioritizing team needs and providing resources for success can shift her focus from control to support. Reflecting on team successes and giving credit where it's due further reinforces this empowering approach.

Case Study 3: Managing a Narcissistic Leadership Style for Team Success

1. How can Liam recognize and address the negative psychological impact of his leadership style on the team?

Liam should seek honest feedback through tools like anonymous surveys or one-on-one meetings to understand how his behavior affects the team. Reflecting on this feedback, he can work to shift his focus from self-promotion to fostering a team-oriented culture. Practicing empathy and recognizing individual contributions are crucial.

2. What steps can Liam take to ensure his leadership emphasizes team contributions and shared success?

Liam can publicly acknowledge and celebrate team achievements, highlighting individual efforts during meetings or in organizational communications. Sharing decision-making responsibilities with team members and giving them visibility in important forums demonstrates that their contributions are valued and appreciated.

3. How can Liam balance his need for recognition with fostering a collaborative and supportive workplace culture?

Liam can redirect his desire for recognition into being known as a leader who builds strong teams and empowers others. He should actively work to create an environment where team success takes precedence over individual accolades. Seeking mentorship or coaching can help Liam further refine his leadership approach.

Appendix 5-A: Answers and Insights for Chapter 5 Case Studies

Case Study 1: Clarifying Role Definitions to Resolve Role Conflict

1. How can Michael analyze and clarify the roles and responsibilities of Sarah and James to resolve this conflict?

Michael can start by conducting individual conversations with Sarah and James to understand their current perceptions of their roles and responsibilities. By identifying overlapping duties and pinpointing areas of ambiguity, he can determine where adjustments are needed. Using tools like a RACI matrix (Responsible, Accountable, Consulted, Informed) can help formally document and delineate responsibilities to ensure clarity.

2. What strategies can Michael use to ensure all team members have a clear understanding of their own and others' roles?

Michael should hold a team-wide meeting to communicate any clarified roles and responsibilities, fostering transparency and ensuring alignment. He can follow up with documentation, such as a responsibility chart, and encourage open communication for feedback on potential conflicts. Periodic reviews of roles during team check-ins can help adapt to any evolving needs.

3. How can defining roles improve team cohesion and reduce future misunderstandings?

Clear roles reduce misunderstandings by ensuring everyone knows their responsibilities and how they fit into the larger team goals. This fosters accountability and trust among team members, minimizing potential friction. With less energy spent on resolving avoidable conflicts, the team can focus on collaboration and productivity, improving overall cohesion.

Case Study 2: Building Psychological Safety to Strengthen Team Collaboration

1. What steps can Maria take to create an environment where team members feel comfortable sharing their ideas and concerns?

Maria should actively model vulnerability by sharing her own experiences and encouraging others to do the same. Establishing ground rules for communication, such as mutual respect and no interruptions, ensures everyone feels safe to contribute. Providing anonymous channels for feedback may help initially hesitant members to share ideas.

2. How might Maria address past behaviors or cultural norms within the team that have discouraged openness?

Maria can acknowledge past issues openly and frame them as opportunities for growth. Inviting team members to participate in structured discussions or retrospectives about these behaviors helps reset norms. She should commit to addressing any lingering effects of these behaviors and hold herself accountable for reinforcing positive changes.

3. What benefits can psychological safety bring to team dynamics and project outcomes?

Psychological safety leads to greater collaboration, creativity, and innovation by encouraging team members to share ideas without fear. It reduces the likelihood of unresolved conflicts and increases trust within the team. This creates a supportive work environment where team members feel empowered to take risks, solve problems, and work toward shared goals.

Case Study 3: Facilitating Creative Conflict for Innovative Solutions

1. How can Emma use facilitation techniques to guide the team's conflict toward productive collaboration?

Emma can introduce structured methods such as the Six Thinking Hats framework, which encourages team members to explore ideas from multiple perspectives without personal bias. Setting time limits for discussions or using a neutral mediator can help maintain focus and reduce emotional tension during brainstorming.

2. What strategies can Emma implement to ensure that differing perspectives are valued and integrated into the final decision?

Emma should emphasize the value of each perspective by summarizing and documenting all contributions during discussions. Using tools like decision matrices or voting systems ensures that decisions are made fairly while incorporating diverse ideas. Following up with team members after decisions are made shows that their input is valued.

3. How might managing creative conflict effectively lead to stronger team relationships and more innovative solutions?

When creative conflict is managed effectively, it fosters mutual respect and strengthens relationships as team members learn to navigate disagreements constructively. It also leverages diverse viewpoints to produce more comprehensive and innovative solutions as ideas are evaluated and refined collaboratively.

Appendix 6-A: Answers and Insights for Chapter 6 Case Studies

Case Study 1: Managing Resistance Through Empathy-Driven Change Management

1. How can Lisa use empathy to understand the specific concerns and fears of her team members regarding the new workflow system?

Lisa should engage in active listening during one-on-one or group discussions, allowing team members to express their concerns without judgment. By paraphrasing their worries and asking clarifying questions, she demonstrates that she values their input and seeks to understand their perspective fully.

2. What strategies can Lisa implement to address these concerns while fostering a sense of inclusion and ownership in the change process?

Lisa can involve team members in the implementation process by seeking their feedback on how the system can be adapted to fit their workflow. Establishing pilot teams to test the system and provide suggestions can foster a sense of ownership and reduce resistance. Transparent communication about timelines and support mechanisms, such as training, also alleviates fears.

3. How might Lisa communicate the benefits of the new system in a way that resonates with her team's individual motivations and needs?

Lisa should tailor her messaging to highlight how the system addresses specific pain points, such as reducing repetitive tasks or improving efficiency. Emphasizing long-term benefits and how the change aligns with both team and individual goals ensures the message resonates on a personal level.

Case Study 2: Navigating Power Dynamics and Reinforcing New Norms

1. What steps can Ethan take to address Laura's concerns while maintaining the integrity of the new leadership hierarchy?

Ethan should hold a private conversation with Laura to validate her feelings and explain the reasoning behind the new hierarchy. By emphasizing her value to the team and offering her a mentorship role, Ethan can align her expertise with the organization's goals while reducing her sense of loss in authority.

2. How can Ethan foster an inclusive environment that minimizes power struggles and encourages team collaboration during this transition?

Ethan should encourage open discussions during team meetings, where all members, including Laura, have equal opportunities to contribute. Creating team-building activities that emphasize collaboration over hierarchy helps reinforce a sense of unity. Recognizing collective achievements rather than individual power highlights the team's shared purpose.

3. What techniques can Ethan use to reinforce the new norms and help the team adjust to the changes without further resistance?

Ethan can consistently communicate the benefits of the new hierarchy and model behaviors that reflect its principles. Rewarding behaviors that align with the new structure and addressing noncompliance promptly ensures that the norms are upheld. Regular feedback sessions provide an avenue for the team to voice concerns and adapt as needed.

Case Study 3: Encouraging Self-Reflection to Reduce Defensive Behavior

1. How can David identify the root causes of Sarah's defensive behavior and help her understand its impact on the team dynamic?

David can observe Sarah's reactions during feedback sessions to identify patterns in her defensiveness. Scheduling a non-confrontational one-on-one discussion allows him to explore her perspective and provide specific examples of how her behavior affects the team. Using open-ended questions encourages Sarah to reflect on her actions.

2. What coaching techniques can David use to encourage Sarah to engage in self-reflection and develop greater emotional intelligence?

David can introduce Sarah to journaling or reflective exercises to help her process feedback objectively. Encouraging her to consider how she might approach situations differently promotes accountability. Offering resources, such as workshops on emotional intelligence or providing a mentor, supports her growth in a structured way.

3. How might fostering self-reflection in Sarah contribute to her growth and the team's overall performance?

Self-reflection helps Sarah become more aware of her triggers and develop strategies for managing them. As she grows emotionally, her ability to accept feedback constructively improves, enhancing her relationships with colleagues. This, in turn, fosters a more collaborative team environment, boosting overall performance.

Appendix 7-A: Answers and Insights for Chapter 7 Case Studies

Case Study 1: Overcoming Multitasking Pitfalls to Boost Productivity

1. What steps can Jordan take to reduce the negative impact of multitasking on his productivity and mental clarity?

Jordan should focus on single-tasking, dedicating uninterrupted blocks of time to specific tasks. He can implement time-blocking techniques, allocating periods for emails, meetings, and deep work separately. Reducing interruptions by turning off non-critical notifications also helps maintain focus.

2. How might Jordan restructure his day to prioritize deep work while managing his ongoing responsibilities?

Jordan can adopt the Eisenhower Matrix to categorize tasks by urgency and importance, focusing on high-priority work first.

Scheduling his most cognitively demanding tasks during his peak productivity hours (often in the morning) ensures optimal mental performance. Delegating or scheduling less critical tasks for later in the day preserves energy for strategic thinking.

3. What psychological strategies can Jordan implement to improve his focus and avoid decision fatigue?

Jordan can use mindfulness techniques, such as focused breathing, to regain clarity and prevent his mind from wandering. Establishing decision-making routines, like creating checklists for repetitive tasks, reduces mental strain. Taking short, regular breaks improves focus and prevents burnout.

Case Study 2: Prioritization Challenges in a Multicultural Team

1. How can Anika leverage prioritization techniques to create a shared understanding of team goals and deadlines?

Anika should use SMART goals (Specific, Measurable, Achievable, Relevant, Time-bound) to define team objectives clearly. By breaking down larger goals into manageable tasks with explicit deadlines, she ensures alignment. Tools like shared project management software can visually communicate priorities and progress.

2. What strategies can Anika use to accommodate cultural differences while maintaining efficiency and cohesion?

Anika can hold team discussions to address cultural attitudes toward time management, fostering mutual understanding and agreement on workflows. Implementing cultural intelligence (CQ) principles enables her to adapt her communication and leadership style to meet diverse needs without compromising efficiency.

3. How might fostering open communication and mutual respect improve the team's time management and overall productivity?

Creating an environment where team members feel comfortable discussing challenges enhances collaboration and ensures alignment. Encouraging open feedback loops and regular check-ins allows Anika to address miscommunications promptly. Mutual respect strengthens the team's cohesion and willingness to adapt to shared priorities.

Case Study 3: Delegating Strategically to Manage Cognitive Overload

1. How can Carlos identify tasks that can be delegated without compromising quality or control?

Carlos can categorize his tasks by complexity and criticality. Routine or repetitive tasks, such as administrative work, can be delegated easily. For complex tasks, Carlos should delegate to team members with relevant expertise, providing clear instructions and milestones to ensure quality.

2. What psychological factors might be contributing to Carlos's reluctance to delegate, and how can he address them?

Carlos may fear losing control or worry about his team's competence. Recognizing this as a form of perfectionism or over-responsibility bias, he can reframe delegation as an opportunity for team development rather than a personal failure. Practicing self-awareness and challenging these limiting beliefs helps him overcome resistance.

3. How can Carlos build trust within his team to ensure successful delegation and reduce his cognitive load?

Carlos should invest in relationship-building activities to understand his team's strengths and capabilities better. Regular feedback sessions and celebrating delegated successes build confidence in his team's abilities. Providing autonomy and avoiding micromanagement fosters trust and motivates team members to take ownership.

Appendix 8-A: Answers and Insights for Chapter 8 Case Studies

Case Study 1: Recognizing the Impact of Stress on Decision-Making and Team Dynamics

1. How might chronic stress be impacting Samantha's cognitive clarity and decision-making abilities?

Chronic stress triggers the fight-or-flight response, increasing cortisol levels that impair cognitive functions such as focus, memory, and decision-making. Samantha's rushed decisions and errors are likely a result of reduced prefrontal cortex activity, which is critical for rational thinking and problem-solving.

2. What are the potential ripple effects of Samantha's stress on her team's morale and performance?

Samantha's stress and irritability create a ripple effect, lowering team morale and increasing hesitation to communicate openly. This may lead to reduced collaboration, lower productivity, and increased stress among team members, further compounding the challenges.

3. What strategies can Samantha implement to manage her stress and improve her leadership effectiveness?

Samantha can incorporate stress management practices such as mindfulness meditation, time-blocking for breaks, and delegating non-critical tasks to her team. Seeking support through counseling services or a mentor can provide tools to manage her emotional responses effectively. Clear communication about her needs and limitations can also foster team support.

Case Study 2: Addressing Physical Symptoms of Stress in Leadership

1. How might James's physical symptoms of stress be connected to his mental strain and workload?

James's symptoms, such as headaches and muscle tension, are physical manifestations of chronic stress. Prolonged activation of the stress response disrupts autonomic nervous system balance, causing these physical issues. Fatigue and declining productivity often result from inadequate recovery time and overstimulation.

2. What practices could James adopt to safeguard his health and maintain sustainable productivity?

James should prioritize regular breaks, physical activity such as stretching or walking, and adequate sleep to support recovery. Delegating tasks and adjusting his workload to align with his energy levels can prevent further strain. Incorporating mindfulness or breathing exercises during the day can help manage immediate stress responses.

3. How could prioritizing his well-being positively influence James's leadership and team performance?

When James prioritizes his health, he models self-care for his team, encouraging them to do the same. Improved physical health enhances his mental clarity, emotional resilience, and decision-making, leading to a more effective and approachable leadership style. This shift can inspire trust and productivity within the team.

Case Study 3: Encouraging a Culture of Well-Being in the Workplace

1. What specific steps can Maria take to create a culture that prioritizes mental and physical well-being?

Maria can implement initiatives such as flexible work arrangements, encouraging breaks, and providing access to wellness resources like Employee Assistance Programs (EAPs). Hosting workshops on stress management or mindfulness demonstrates her commitment to well-being.

2. How can Maria encourage her team to adopt healthy work habits without compromising productivity?

Maria can schedule mandatory lunch breaks or "no-meeting zones" to protect downtime. Recognizing and rewarding efficiency rather than overwork encourages healthier habits. Openly discussing the importance of well-being during team meetings normalizes the practice without stigmatizing those who prioritize self-care.

3. What role does modeling self-care play in Maria's ability to lead by example and inspire her team?

By taking breaks, using vacation time, and openly prioritizing her well-being, Maria sets a powerful example. Modeling these behaviors normalizes them, empowering her team to follow suit. This approach builds a culture of balance, reducing burnout while maintaining productivity and long-term success.

Note: For further insights and key terms, refer to the **Glossary** section.

Try This: Actionable Steps for Developing the Project Manager Mindset

There are seven Try This" sections in this book. These sections assist in putting insights from the provided chapters into practice by working as actionable steps and exercises that are designed to help you cultivate the lessons learned from each chapter. These steps align with the principles explored in this book, ensuring you can apply them to real-world scenarios for personal and professional growth.

Self-Assessment

This book consists of three self-assessments. These self-assessments are designed to help you reflect on the key aspects discussed in each chapter (chapters 1-3, 4, and 5). The directions are for you to answer the questions honestly based on your current behaviors, attitudes, and practices. Use the scoring guide and interpretation below to evaluate your results and develop strategies for improvement.

This self-assessment provides a foundation for understanding your current leadership. The idea is for you to revisit this exercise periodically as you progress through the book to track your growth and refine your strategies.

Case Study

At the end of each chapter are case studies. These case studies provide practical, scenario-based applications of the concepts discussed in each chapter, encouraging readers to integrate cognitive restructuring, emotional regulation, emotional contagion techniques, and practicality into their daily leadership practices

Team Diagnostic Survey

The Evaluating Team Dynamics survey is a practical tool to help you understand the health of your team's dynamics. Revisit it regularly to measure progress and refine strategies for fostering a cohesive, high-performing team.

Glossary

Self-Awareness: The conscious knowledge of one's own character, emotions, and motivations. In leadership, self-awareness enhances emotional intelligence and the ability to recognize stress factors.

Continuous Improvement: The ongoing effort to improve processes, services, or products incrementally over time, essential for adaptive leadership in dynamic environments.

Cognitive Flexibility: The ability to shift thinking and adapt strategies in response to changing information. This is vital in navigating complex decision-making scenarios.

Cognitive Inflexibility: The inability to shift or adapt thinking, often resulting in rigid decision-making and potential for resistance to change.

Decision-Making Paralysis: A state of indecision due to overwhelming information or the pressure of making the "perfect" choice, often seen in high-stress environments.

Cognitive Reappraisal: A technique involving the reframing of thoughts about a situation to alter its emotional impact, a common method in stress management and emotional regulation.

Divergent Thinking: The process of generating creative ideas by exploring multiple potential solutions. In leadership, this supports innovative problem-solving and team engagement.

Self-Regulation: The capacity to manage one's own emotions, thoughts, and behaviors in different situations, crucial for maintaining professionalism and calm under pressure.

Social Skills: The ability to interact and communicate effectively with others, an essential component of emotional intelligence and successful leadership.

Psychological Resilience: The ability to mentally recover from or adapt to challenges and adversity, which enables leaders to maintain stability under stress.

Scope: Defines the objectives and boundaries of a project or role. Properly managing scope ensures projects remain focused and aligned with strategic goals.

Employee Assistance Program (EAP) : Organizational resources that provide support for employees dealing with personal or work-related challenges, including counseling services for stress and mental health.

Self-Sabotaging Behaviors: Actions that hinder personal success or progress, often driven by unconscious fears or low self-esteem.

Imposter Syndrome: A psychological pattern where individuals doubt their abilities and fear being exposed as "frauds," despite clear achievements.

Cognitive Distortion: Patterns of negative thinking that distort reality, often leading to stress or negative self-perception. Common types include "black-and-white thinking" and "catastrophizing."

Cognitive Restructuring: The process of identifying and altering negative thought patterns to promote healthier perspectives, often used in stress management and leadership training.

Cognitive-Behavioral Approaches: Techniques derived from cognitive-behavioral therapy (CBT) that focus on changing thought patterns to influence behaviors and emotions.

Cognitive Reappraisal: An emotional regulation strategy where one reassesses a situation to change its emotional impact, useful in managing stress reactions.

Emotional Regulation: The ability to manage and respond to emotional experiences in a balanced way, preventing impulsive reactions in high-stakes situations.

Entrenched Behavioral Patterns: Deeply ingrained habits or responses that can be resistant to change, often requiring focused effort to modify.

Cognitive Behavioral Therapy (CBT) : A psychological treatment aimed at identifying and challenging cognitive distortions to improve emotional and behavioral responses.

Reframing: Changing the way a situation or information is interpreted to alter its emotional impact, supporting resilience and adaptability.

Emotional Regulation Theory: A framework for understanding how individuals influence their emotional states, including strategies for enhancing emotional control.

Interpersonal Conflict: Disagreements or clashes between individuals, often due to differences in values, goals, or communication styles, which can impact team cohesion.

Emotional Contagion: The phenomenon of emotions spreading from one person to another, with leaders often setting the emotional tone within a team.

Empathy: The ability to understand and share another person's feelings, a core component of effective communication and leadership

Sympathy: Feelings of pity and sorrow for someone else's misfortune, distinct from empathy as it involves a more removed, externalized response.

Prefrontal Cortex: The part of the brain responsible for complex cognitive functions, including decision-making, which is impacted by prolonged stress.

Victim Mentality: A mindset where individuals view themselves as victims of circumstance, often resulting in a lack of personal accountability and agency.

Deflection: A defense mechanism where individuals avoid addressing issues by shifting focus away from themselves, often seen in conflict management scenarios.

Change Readiness: An individual or organization's willingness and preparedness to adapt to new conditions, vital for managing transitions and innovation.

Social Proof: The psychological tendency to align with the behaviors or beliefs of others, often utilized in leadership to encourage positive cultural norms.

Social Conformity: The practice of adjusting behaviors or beliefs to match those of a group, often affecting team dynamics and decision-making.

Defensive Behavior: Reactions intended to protect oneself from perceived criticism or threat, which can disrupt open communication and collaborative work.

Germane Load: The mental effort directed at learning or understanding core content, as opposed to unnecessary or distracting information.

Chunking: A strategy of breaking down information into manageable parts to facilitate comprehension and memory retention.

Mind Reading: Assuming to know what others are thinking, especially if negative, often without evidence. This cognitive distortion can lead to unnecessary stress or interpersonal tension.

Affective Forecasting: Predicting one's emotional reaction to future events, which is often inaccurate due to cognitive biases.

Agility: The ability of an organization or individual to adapt swiftly and effectively to changes, essential for competitive advantage.

Anchoring Bias: The cognitive bias where initial information disproportionately influences decisions, even if it's irrelevant.

Autonomy: The degree of independence individuals or teams have in making decisions, impacting motivation and accountability.

Behavioral Economics: A field combining psychology and economics to understand how cognitive factors influence decision-making.

Bias for Action: A leadership trait favoring proactive decision-making and problem-solving, promoting productivity and responsiveness.

Cognitive Dissonance: The discomfort from holding contradictory beliefs or values, often driving efforts to resolve the inconsistency.

Cultural Intelligence (CQ) : The capability to function effectively across various cultural contexts, critical in diverse team settings.

Decision Fatigue: The decline in decision quality after prolonged decision-making, often leading to impulsivity or avoidance.

Disruptive Innovation: Innovations that drastically alter industries or markets, requiring adaptive leadership to manage transitions.

Distributed Team: A team whose members are spread across different locations, requiring advanced communication and collaboration skills.

Engagement: The level of enthusiasm and dedication an employee feels towards their work, directly influencing performance and retention.

Executive Function: Cognitive abilities such as memory, flexibility, and self-control, which are essential for effective leadership.

Fight-or-Flight Response: The body's automatic reaction to perceived threats, a physiological mechanism that can lead to burnout if chronically activated.

Flow State: A mental state where an individual is fully engaged in an activity, resulting in high productivity and satisfaction.

Groupthink: The tendency for consensus-seeking within a group to suppress dissent, often leading to poor decision-making.

Growth Mindset: The belief that skills and abilities can develop through effort, fostering resilience and adaptability.

Implicit Bias: Unconscious attitudes that influence perceptions and decisions, impacting diversity and inclusion efforts.

Introspection: Examining one's own thoughts and feelings, essential for recognizing personal stressors or biases.

Key Performance Indicators (KPIs): Metrics used to evaluate the success of an organization or team in achieving strategic objectives.

Leadership Agility: The capacity to make timely, effective decisions in dynamic conditions, essential for leading through change.

Multicultural Competence: The ability to work effectively with individuals from diverse backgrounds, a crucial skill for modern leaders.

Neuroplasticity: The brain's ability to reorganize and adapt, fundamental for learning and personal development.

Nudging: Influencing decision-making subtly through indirect suggestions, often used in behavioral economics.

Organizational Resilience: The ability to prepare for and adapt to incremental changes and disruptions, supporting sustainable performance.

Projection Bias: Overestimating how much future preferences align with present ones, often affecting long-term planning.

Rumination: Persistent focus on distressing events or thoughts, a habit that can contribute to chronic stress.

Role Ambiguity: Uncertainty about job expectations, leading to stress and decreased productivity.

Self-Efficacy: One's belief in their ability to achieve goals, influencing motivation and perseverance.

Situational Awareness: Perceiving, interpreting, and responding accurately to dynamic environments, essential for effective decision-making.

Sunk Cost Fallacy: Continuing an endeavor due to prior investment, even if it's no longer beneficial, often seen in project management.

Transactional Leadership: A management style focused on structured tasks and rewards, effective in routine-driven environments.

Transformational Leadership: A style that inspires others to achieve personal and professional growth through shared vision and goals.

Trust Radius: The level of trust extended within a team, impacting collaboration and communication.

Value Alignment: The alignment of individual and organizational values fostering commitment and purpose within a team.

Vicarious Trauma: Emotional impact from exposure to others' traumatic experiences, relevant for leaders in high-stress fields.

Wellness Programs: Initiatives aimed at improving employee health and reducing stress, enhancing resilience and productivity.

Workplace Culture: The shared beliefs and values within an organization that shape employee behavior and engagement.

www.ingramcontent.com/pod-product-compliance
Lightning Source LLC
Chambersburg PA
CBHW020925090426
42736CB00010B/1041